MATH GAMES
The Dice Game

Copyright © 2019 by Kitty Learning

The Dice Game

Roll two dice. Add the numbers together, or subtract the smaller number from the larger number. Can you find your answer below? Color it in. Can you get four in a row?

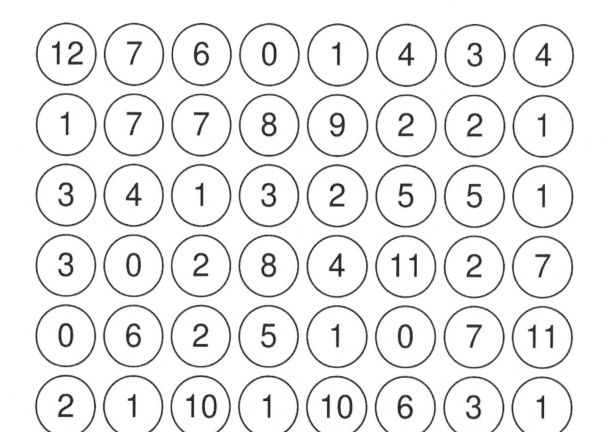

12 7 6 0 1 4 3 4

1 7 7 8 9 2 2 1

3 4 1 3 2 5 5 1

3 0 2 8 4 11 2 7

0 6 2 5 1 0 7 11

2 1 10 1 10 6 3 1

The Dice Game

Roll two dice. Add the numbers together, or subtract the smaller number from the larger number. Can you find your answer below? Color it in. Can you get four in a row?

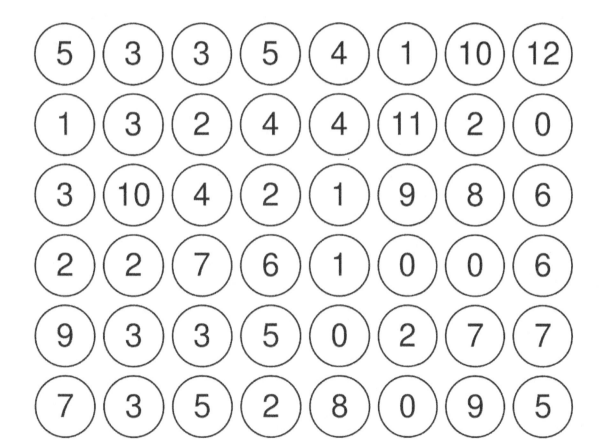

The Dice Game

Roll two dice. Add the numbers together, or subtract the smaller number from the larger number. Can you find your answer below? Color it in. Can you get four in a row?

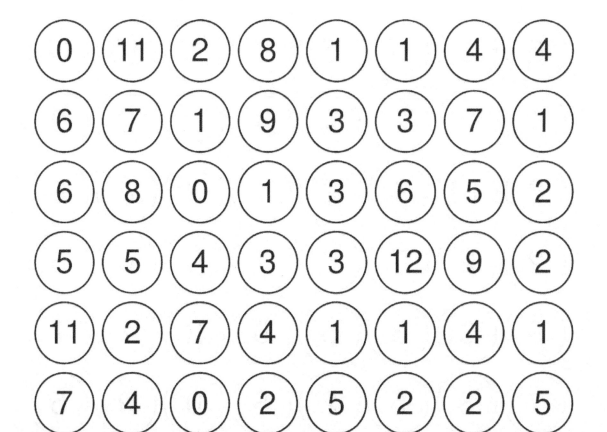

The Dice Game

Roll two dice. Add the numbers together, or subtract the smaller number from the larger number. Can you find your answer below? Color it in. Can you get four in a row?

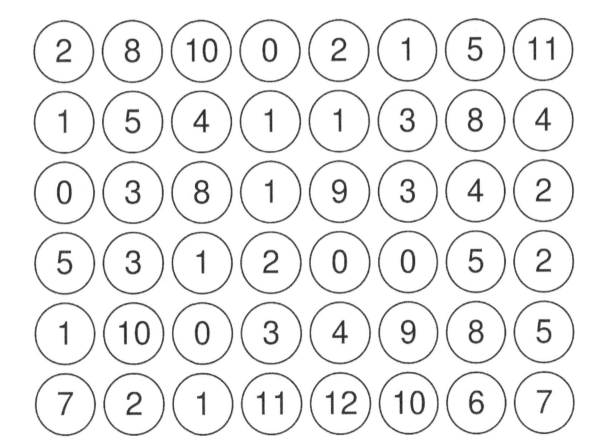

2	8	10	0	2	1	5	11
1	5	4	1	1	3	8	4
0	3	8	1	9	3	4	2
5	3	1	2	0	0	5	2
1	10	0	3	4	9	8	5
7	2	1	11	12	10	6	7

Name _____ Date _____

The Dice Game

Roll two dice. Add the numbers together, or subtract the smaller number from the larger number. Can you find your answer below? Color it in. Can you get four in a row?

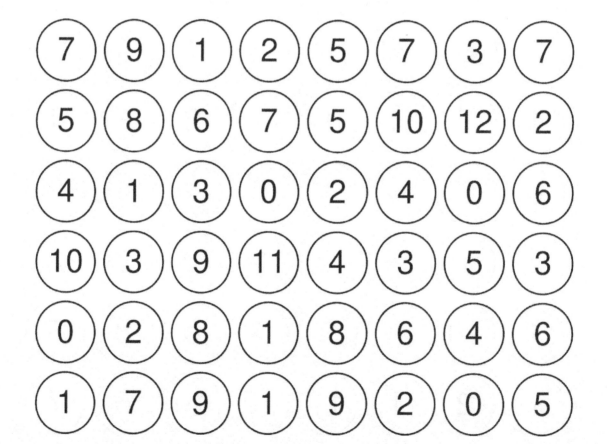

7	9	1	2	5	7	3	7
5	8	6	7	5	10	12	2
4	1	3	0	2	4	0	6
10	3	9	11	4	3	5	3
0	2	8	1	8	6	4	6
1	7	9	1	9	2	0	5

Name _____   Date _____

The Dice Game

Roll two dice. Add the numbers together, or subtract the smaller number from the larger number. Can you find your answer below? Color it in. Can you get four in a row?

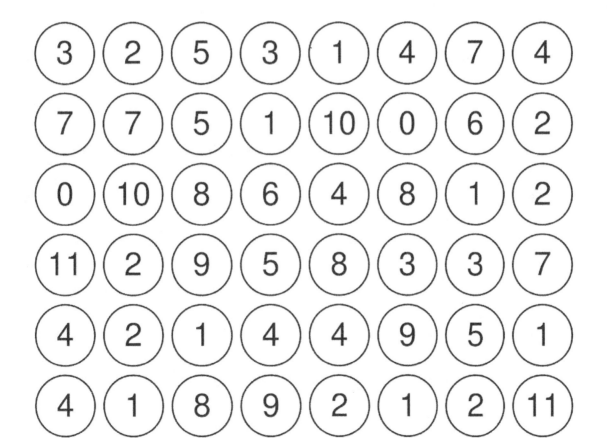

The Dice Game

Roll two dice. Add the numbers together, or subtract the smaller number from the larger number. Can you find your answer below? Color it in. Can you get four in a row?

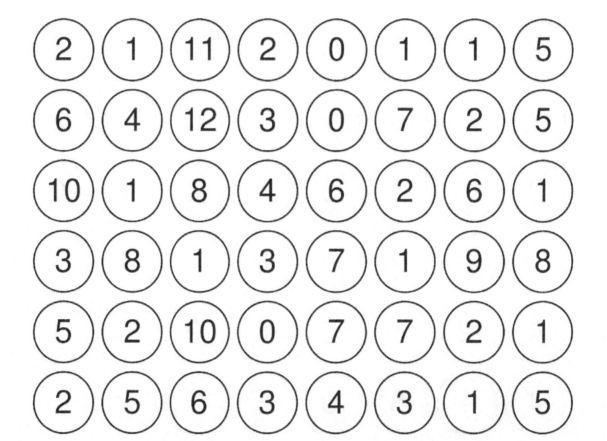

2	1	11	2	0	1	1	5
6	4	12	3	0	7	2	5
10	1	8	4	6	2	6	1
3	8	1	3	7	1	9	8
5	2	10	0	7	7	2	1
2	5	6	3	4	3	1	5

The Dice Game

Roll two dice. Add the numbers together, or subtract the smaller number from the larger number. Can you find your answer below? Color it in. Can you get four in a row?

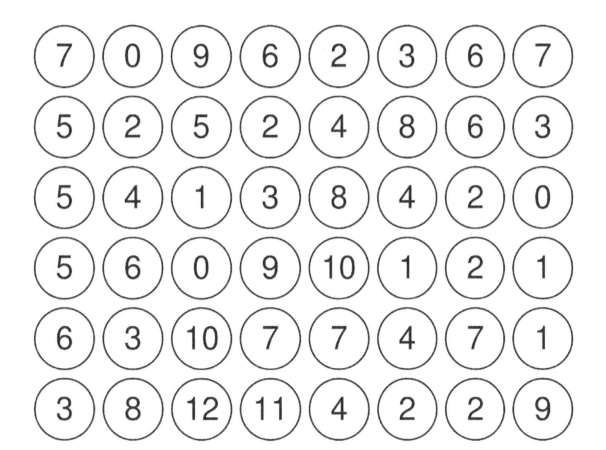

Name _____ Date _____

The Dice Game

Roll two dice. Add the
numbers together, or
subtract the smaller number
from the larger number.
Can you find your answer
below? Color it in. Can you
get four in a row?

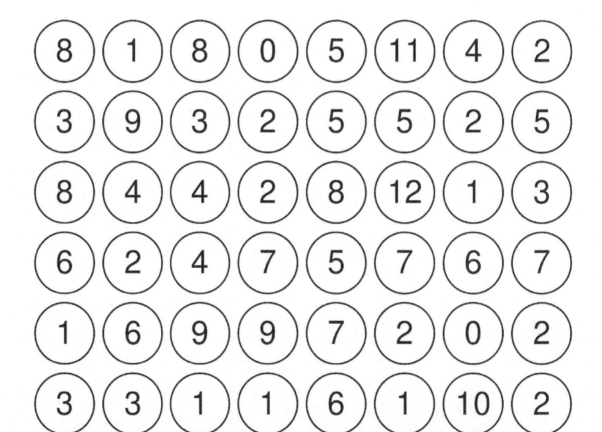

8	1	8	0	5	11	4	2
3	9	3	2	5	5	2	5
8	4	4	2	8	12	1	3
6	2	4	7	5	7	6	7
1	6	9	9	7	2	0	2
3	3	1	1	6	1	10	2

The Dice Game

Roll two dice. Add the numbers together, or subtract the smaller number from the larger number. Can you find your answer below? Color it in. Can you get four in a row?

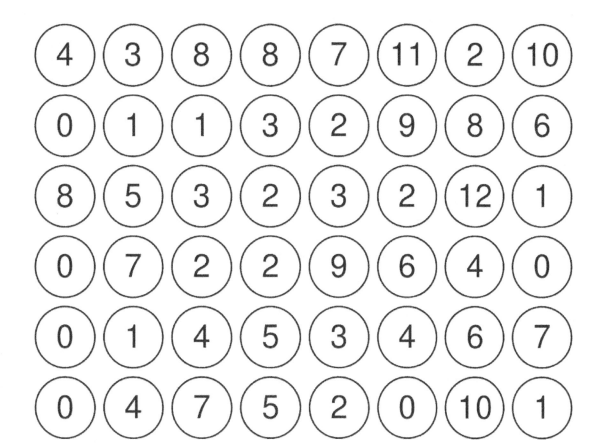

The Dice Game

Roll two dice. Add the numbers together, or subtract the smaller number from the larger number. Can you find your answer below? Color it in. Can you get four in a row?

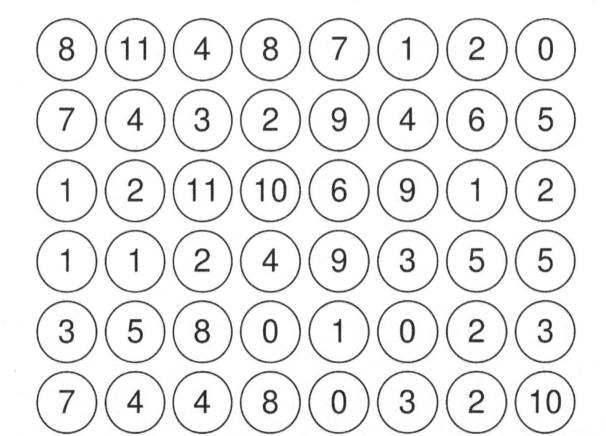

8	11	4	8	7	1	2	0
7	4	3	2	9	4	6	5
1	2	11	10	6	9	1	2
1	1	2	4	9	3	5	5
3	5	8	0	1	0	2	3
7	4	4	8	0	3	2	10

The Dice Game

Roll two dice. Add the numbers together, or subtract the smaller number from the larger number. Can you find your answer below? Color it in. Can you get four in a row?

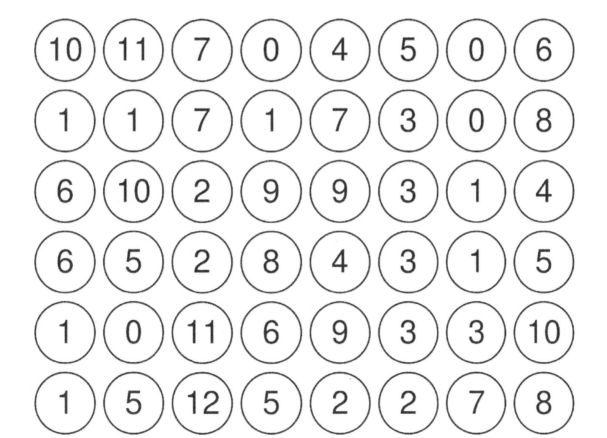

10 11 7 0 4 5 0 6

1 1 7 1 7 3 0 8

6 10 2 9 9 3 1 4

6 5 2 8 4 3 1 5

1 0 11 6 9 3 3 10

1 5 12 5 2 2 7 8

The Dice Game

Roll two dice. Add the numbers together, or subtract the smaller number from the larger number. Can you find your answer below? Color it in. Can you get four in a row?

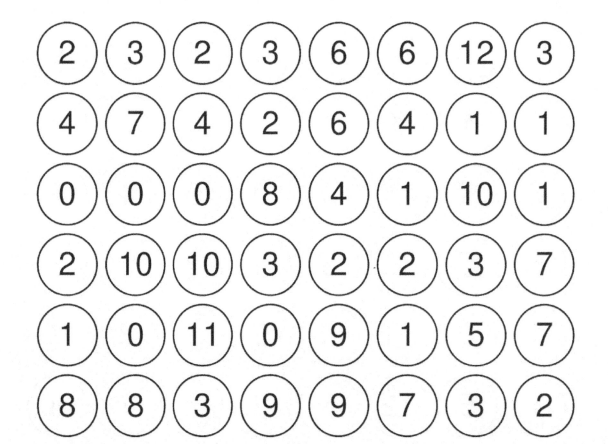

The Dice Game

Roll two dice. Add the numbers together, or subtract the smaller number from the larger number. Can you find your answer below? Color it in. Can you get four in a row?

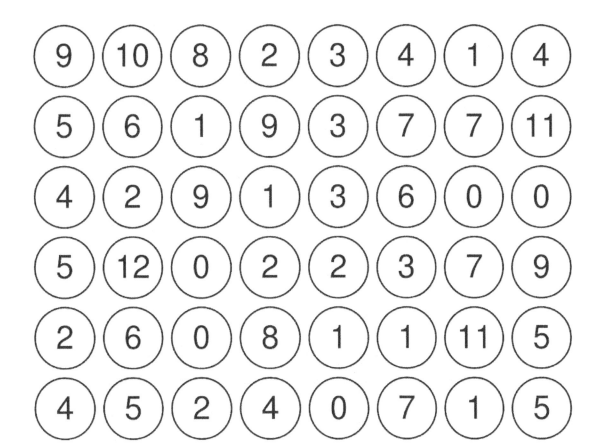

The Dice Game

Roll two dice. Add the numbers together, or subtract the smaller number from the larger number. Can you find your answer below? Color it in. Can you get four in a row?

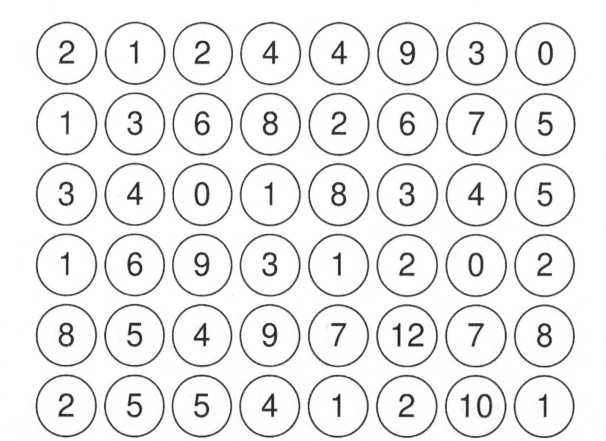

Name _____ Date _____

The Dice Game

Roll two dice. Add the numbers together, or subtract the smaller number from the larger number. Can you find your answer below? Color it in. Can you get four in a row?

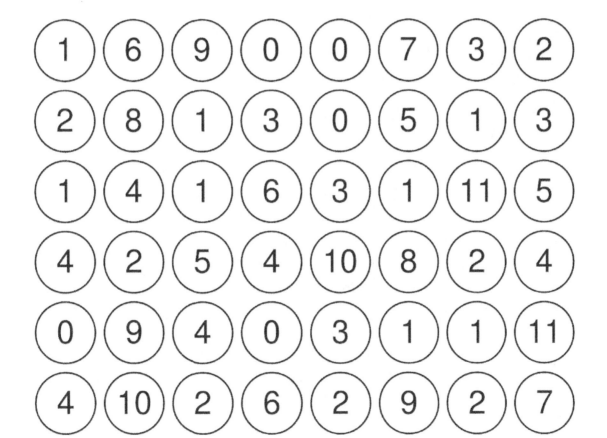

1	6	9	0	0	7	3	2
2	8	1	3	0	5	1	3
1	4	1	6	3	1	11	5
4	2	5	4	10	8	2	4
0	9	4	0	3	1	1	11
4	10	2	6	2	9	2	7

The Dice Game

Roll two dice. Add the numbers together, or subtract the smaller number from the larger number. Can you find your answer below? Color it in. Can you get four in a row?

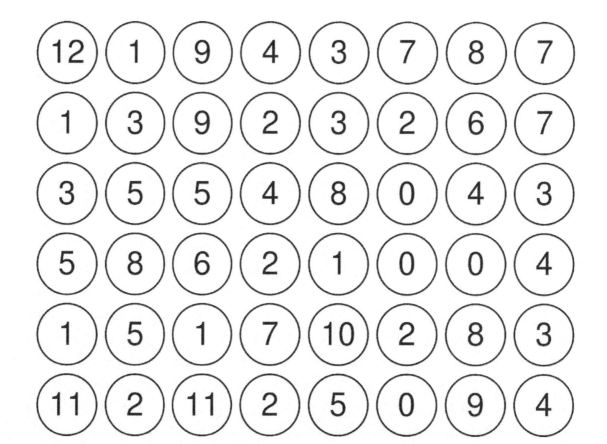

12	1	9	4	3	7	8	7
1	3	9	2	3	2	6	7
3	5	5	4	8	0	4	3
5	8	6	2	1	0	0	4
1	5	1	7	10	2	8	3
11	2	11	2	5	0	9	4

The Dice Game

Roll two dice. Add the numbers together, or subtract the smaller number from the larger number. Can you find your answer below? Color it in. Can you get four in a row?

9	5	3	8	5	11	2	1
2	9	1	1	3	1	7	11
1	5	2	4	8	1	10	3
4	3	6	1	12	7	7	9
8	7	0	10	5	0	4	8
5	3	4	4	0	6	1	6

The Dice Game

Roll two dice. Add the numbers together, or subtract the smaller number from the larger number. Can you find your answer below? Color it in. Can you get four in a row?

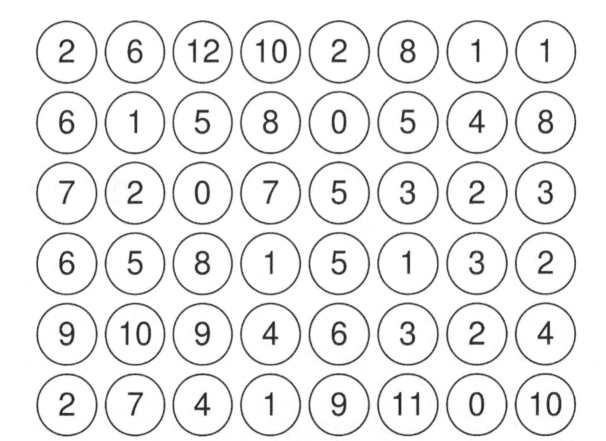

The Dice Game

Roll two dice. Add the numbers together, or subtract the smaller number from the larger number. Can you find your answer below? Color it in. Can you get four in a row?

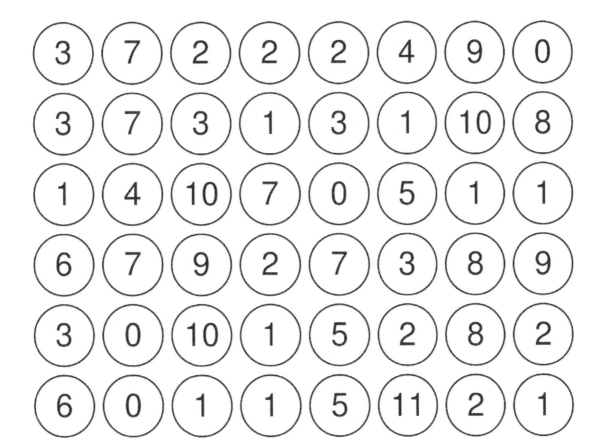

The Dice Game

Roll two dice. Add the numbers together, or subtract the smaller number from the larger number. Can you find your answer below? Color it in. Can you get four in a row?

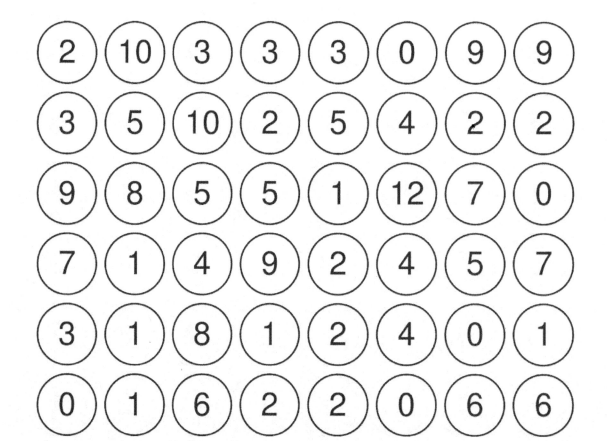

The Dice Game

Roll two dice. Add the numbers together, or subtract the smaller number from the larger number. Can you find your answer below? Color it in. Can you get four in a row?

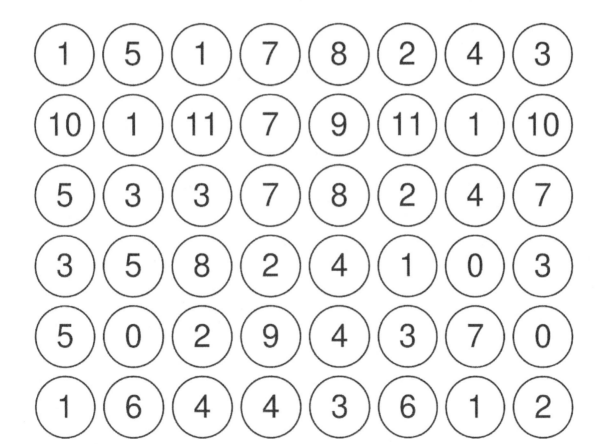

The Dice Game

Roll two dice. Add the numbers together, or subtract the smaller number from the larger number. Can you find your answer below? Color it in. Can you get four in a row?

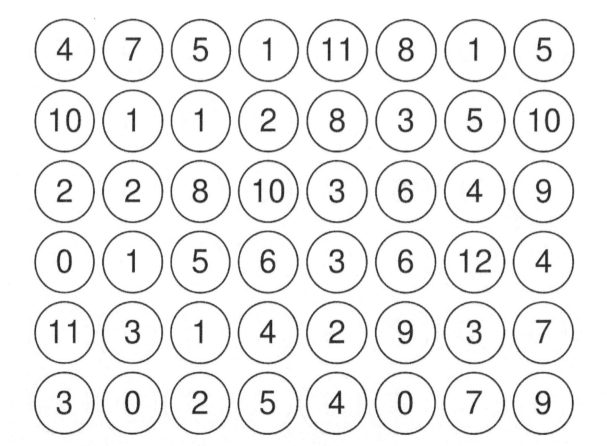

The Dice Game

Roll two dice. Add the numbers together, or subtract the smaller number from the larger number. Can you find your answer below? Color it in. Can you get four in a row?

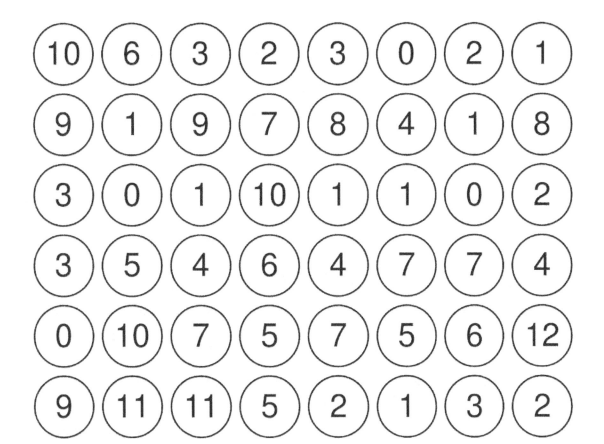

The Dice Game

Roll two dice. Add the numbers together, or subtract the smaller number from the larger number. Can you find your answer below? Color it in. Can you get four in a row?

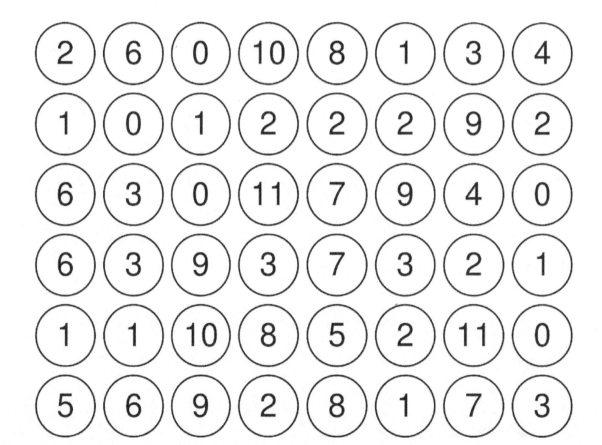

The Dice Game

Roll three dice. Start with the number on one of the dice. Add or subtract the numbers on each of the other dice. Can you find your answer below? Color it in. Can you get four in a row?

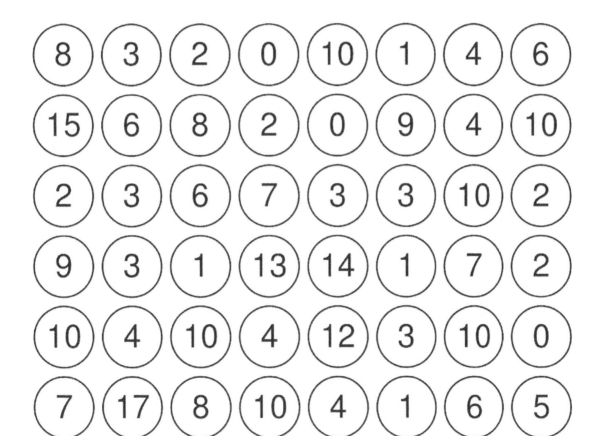

The Dice Game

Roll three dice. Start with the number on one of the dice. Add or subtract the numbers on each of the other dice. Can you find your answer below? Color it in. Can you get four in a row?

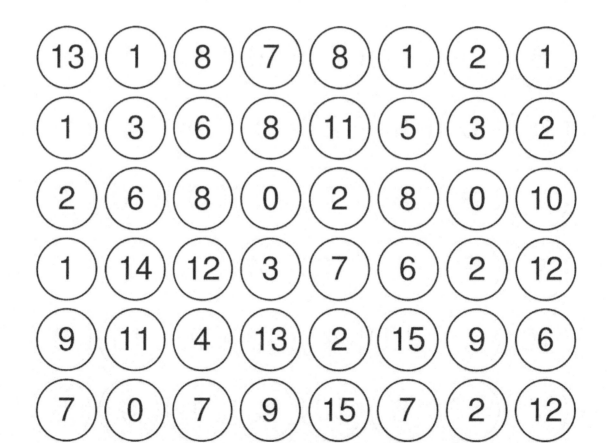

The Dice Game

Roll three dice. Start with the number on one of the dice. Add or subtract the numbers on each of the other dice. Can you find your answer below? Color it in. Can you get four in a row?

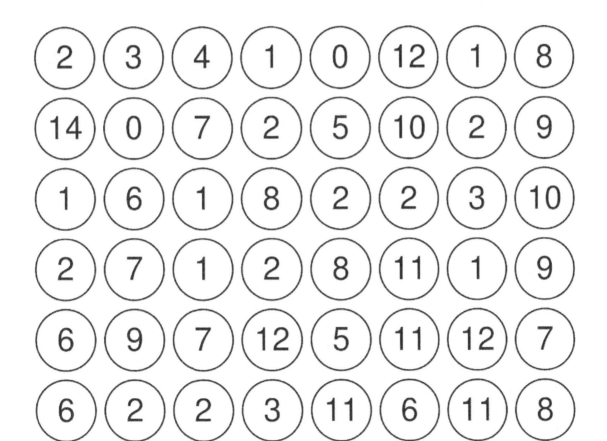

2　3　4　1　0　12　1　8

14　0　7　2　5　10　2　9

1　6　1　8　2　2　3　10

2　7　1　2　8　11　1　9

6　9　7　12　5　11　12　7

6　2　2　3　11　6　11　8

The Dice Game

Roll three dice. Start with the number on one of the dice. Add or subtract the numbers on each of the other dice. Can you find your answer below? Color it in. Can you get four in a row?

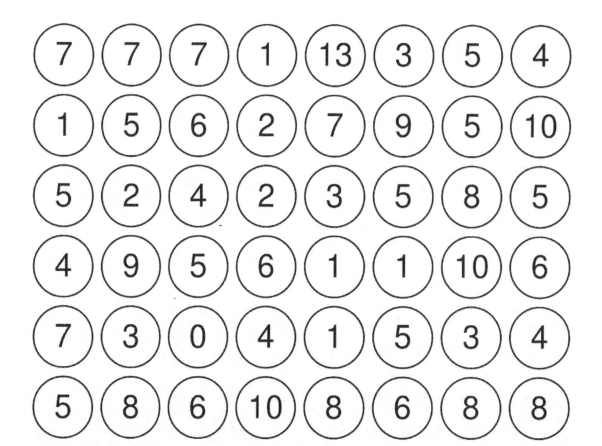

The Dice Game

Roll three dice. Start with the number on one of the dice. Add or subtract the numbers on each of the other dice. Can you find your answer below? Color it in. Can you get four in a row?

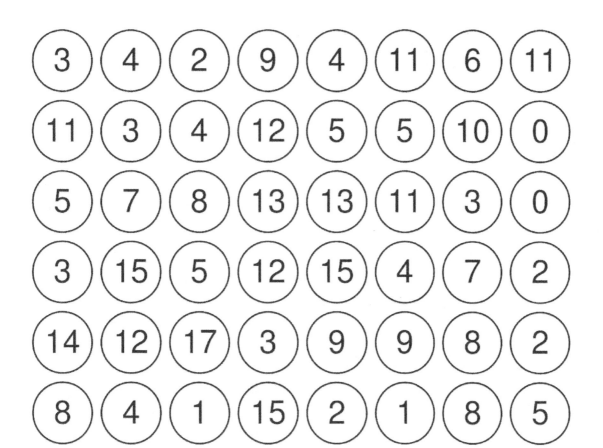

3	4	2	9	4	11	6	11
11	3	4	12	5	5	10	0
5	7	8	13	13	11	3	0
3	15	5	12	15	4	7	2
14	12	17	3	9	9	8	2
8	4	1	15	2	1	8	5

The Dice Game

Roll three dice. Start with the number on one of the dice. Add or subtract the numbers on each of the other dice. Can you find your answer below? Color it in. Can you get four in a row?

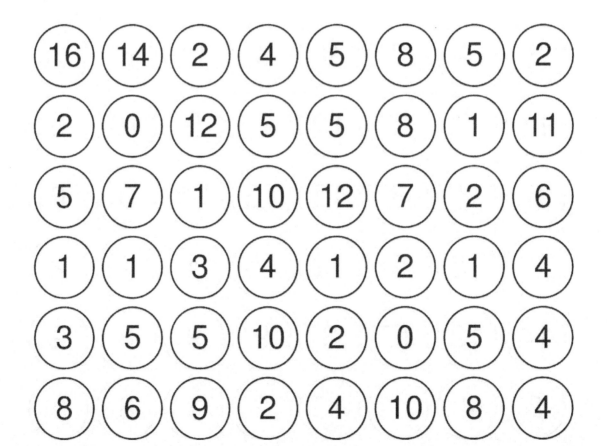

16 14 2 4 5 8 5 2

2 0 12 5 5 8 1 11

5 7 1 10 12 7 2 6

1 1 3 4 1 2 1 4

3 5 5 10 2 0 5 4

8 6 9 2 4 10 8 4

The Dice Game

Roll three dice. Start with the number on one of the dice. Add or subtract the numbers on each of the other dice. Can you find your answer below? Color it in. Can you get four in a row?

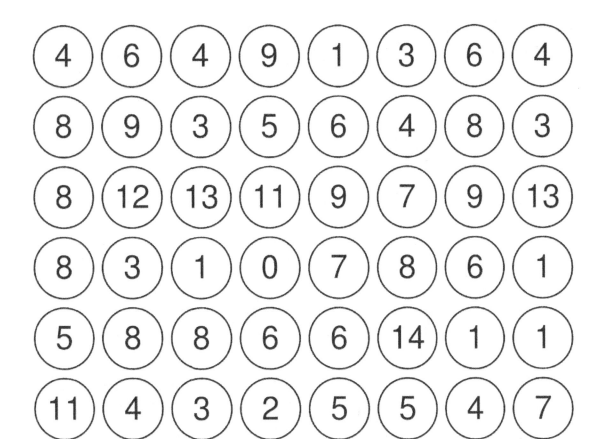

The Dice Game

Roll three dice. Start with the number on one of the dice. Add or subtract the numbers on each of the other dice. Can you find your answer below? Color it in. Can you get four in a row?

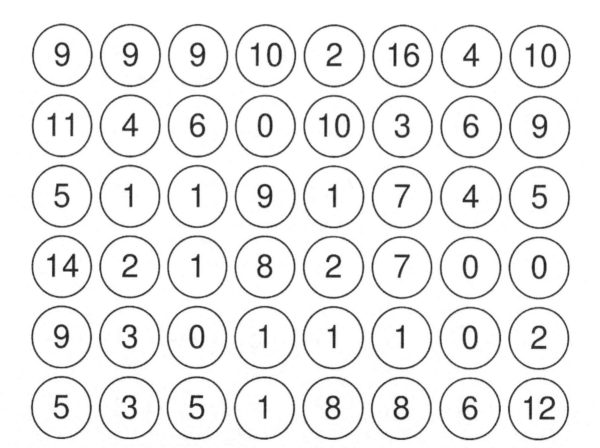

9	9	9	10	2	16	4	10
11	4	6	0	10	3	6	9
5	1	1	9	1	7	4	5
14	2	1	8	2	7	0	0
9	3	0	1	1	1	0	2
5	3	5	1	8	8	6	12

The Dice Game

Roll three dice. Start with the number on one of the dice. Add or subtract the numbers on each of the other dice. Can you find your answer below? Color it in. Can you get four in a row?

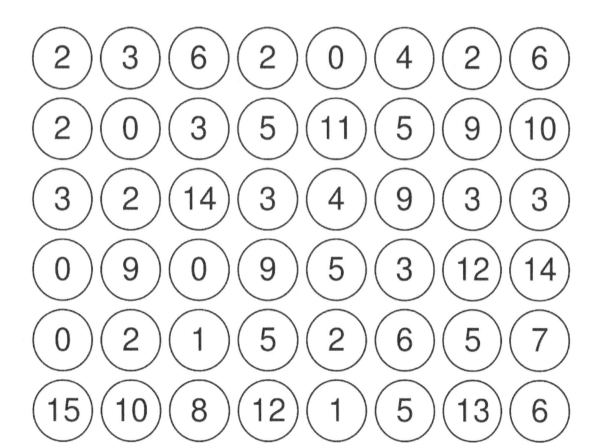

2	3	6	2	0	4	2	6
2	0	3	5	11	5	9	10
3	2	14	3	4	9	3	3
0	9	0	9	5	3	12	14
0	2	1	5	2	6	5	7
15	10	8	12	1	5	13	6

The Dice Game

Roll three dice. Start with the number on one of the dice. Add or subtract the numbers on each of the other dice. Can you find your answer below? Color it in. Can you get four in a row?

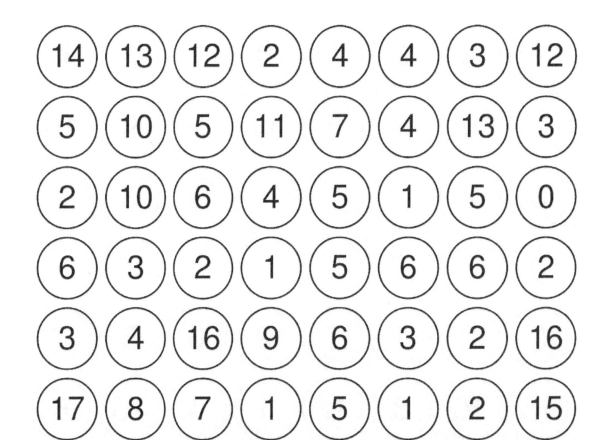

14	13	12	2	4	4	3	12
5	10	5	11	7	4	13	3
2	10	6	4	5	1	5	0
6	3	2	1	5	6	6	2
3	4	16	9	6	3	2	16
17	8	7	1	5	1	2	15

The Dice Game

Roll three dice. Start with the number on one of the dice. Add or subtract the numbers on each of the other dice. Can you find your answer below? Color it in. Can you get four in a row?

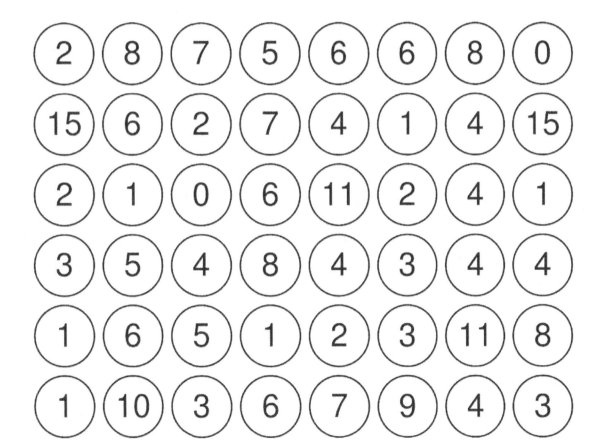

The Dice Game

Roll three dice. Start with the number on one of the dice. Add or subtract the numbers on each of the other dice. Can you find your answer below? Color it in. Can you get four in a row?

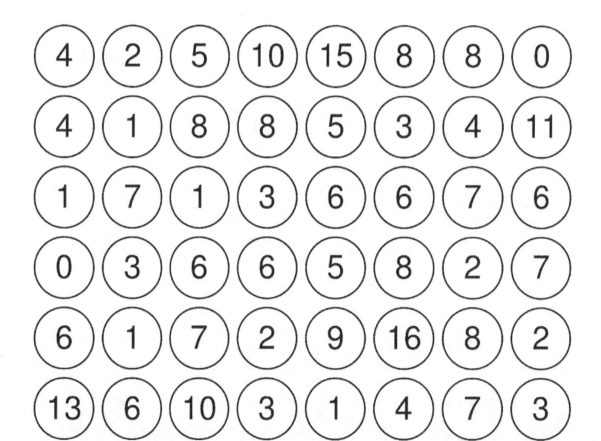

The Dice Game

Roll three dice. Start with the number on one of the dice. Add or subtract the numbers on each of the other dice. Can you find your answer below? Color it in. Can you get four in a row?

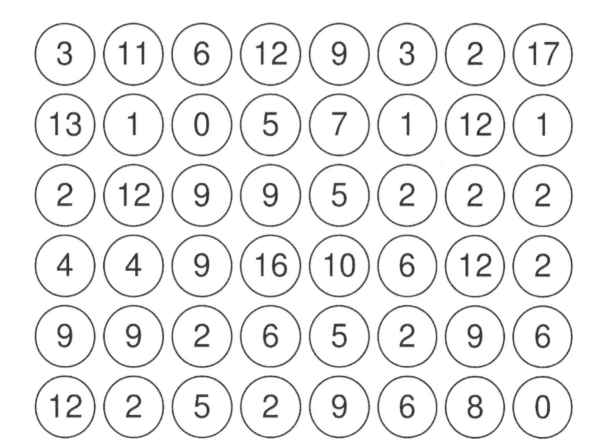

The Dice Game

Roll three dice. Start with the number on one of the dice. Add or subtract the numbers on each of the other dice. Can you find your answer below? Color it in. Can you get four in a row?

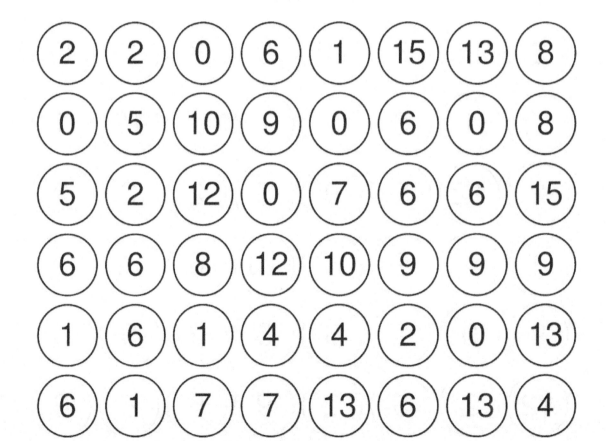

The Dice Game

Roll three dice. Start with the number on one of the dice. Add or subtract the numbers on each of the other dice. Can you find your answer below? Color it in. Can you get four in a row?

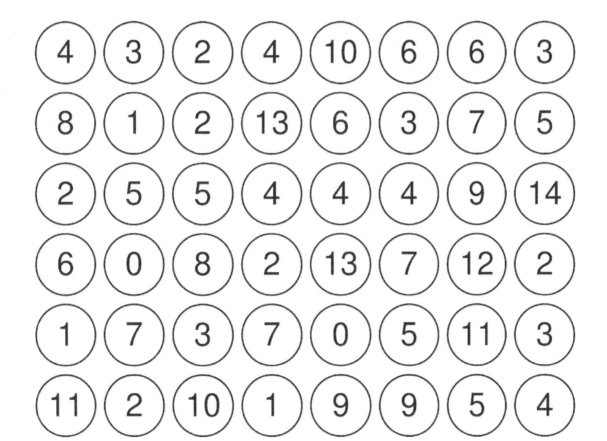

The Dice Game

Roll three dice. Start with the number on one of the dice. Add or subtract the numbers on each of the other dice. Can you find your answer below? Color it in. Can you get four in a row?

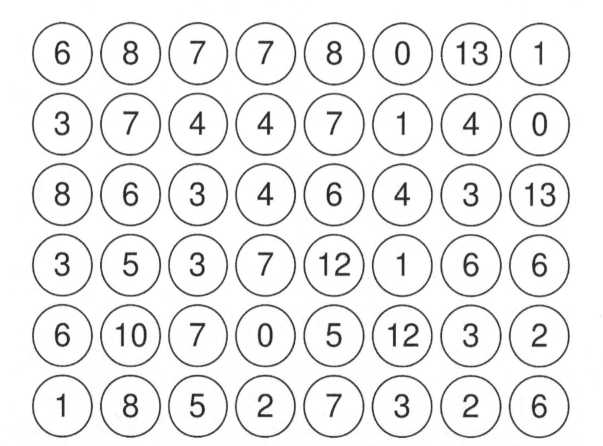

The Dice Game

Roll three dice. Start with the number on one of the dice. Add or subtract the numbers on each of the other dice. Can you find your answer below? Color it in. Can you get four in a row?

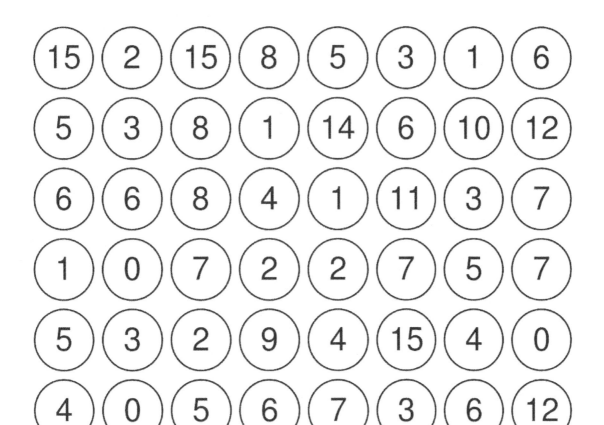

15 2 15 8 5 3 1 6

5 3 8 1 14 6 10 12

6 6 8 4 1 11 3 7

1 0 7 2 2 7 5 7

5 3 2 9 4 15 4 0

4 0 5 6 7 3 6 12

The Dice Game

Roll three dice. Start with the number on one of the dice. Add or subtract the numbers on each of the other dice. Can you find your answer below? Color it in. Can you get four in a row?

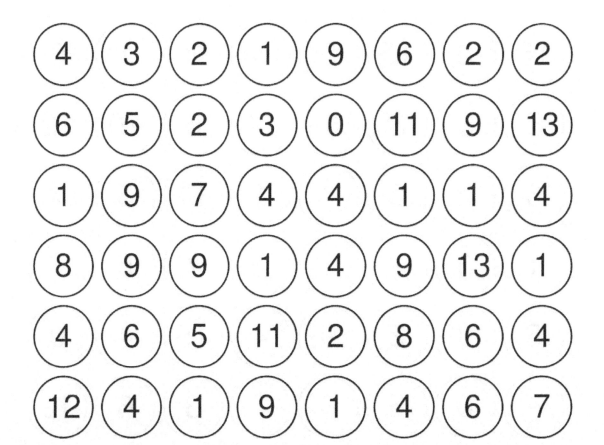

The Dice Game

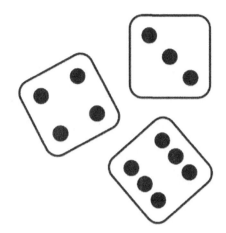

Roll three dice. Start with the number on one of the dice. Add or subtract the numbers on each of the other dice. Can you find your answer below? Color it in. Can you get four in a row?

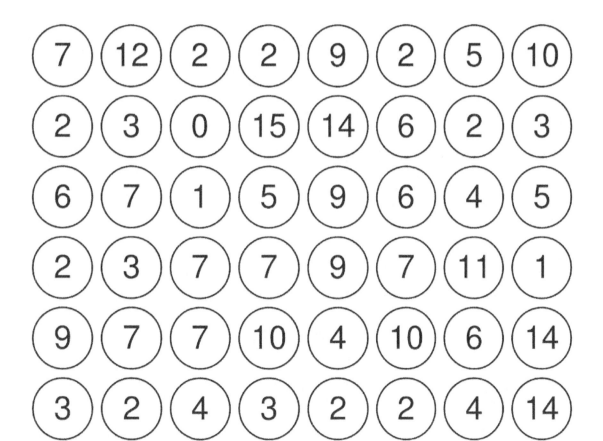

7	12	2	2	9	2	5	10
2	3	0	15	14	6	2	3
6	7	1	5	9	6	4	5
2	3	7	7	9	7	11	1
9	7	7	10	4	10	6	14
3	2	4	3	2	2	4	14

Name _____ Date _____

The Dice Game

Roll three dice. Start with the number on one of the dice. Add or subtract the numbers on each of the other dice. Can you find your answer below? Color it in. Can you get four in a row?

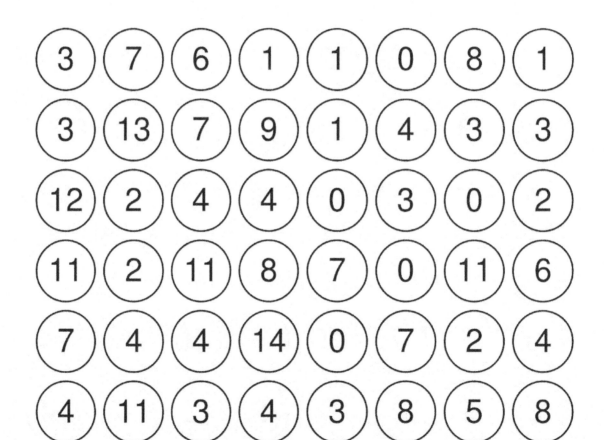

3	7	6	1	1	0	8	1
3	13	7	9	1	4	3	3
12	2	4	4	0	3	0	2
11	2	11	8	7	0	11	6
7	4	4	14	0	7	2	4
4	11	3	4	3	8	5	8

The Dice Game

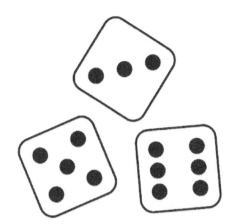

Roll three dice. Start with the number on one of the dice. Add or subtract the numbers on each of the other dice. Can you find your answer below? Color it in. Can you get four in a row?

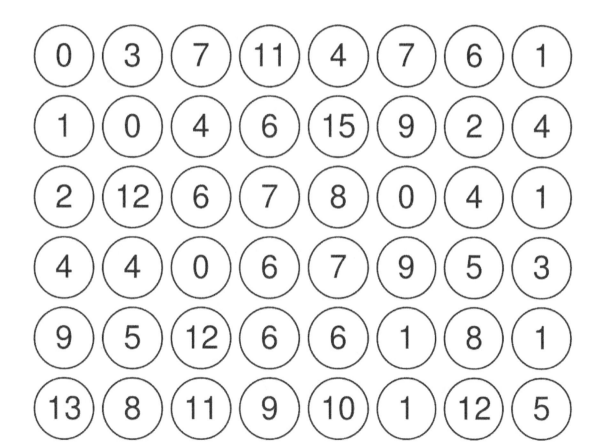

0	3	7	11	4	7	6	1
1	0	4	6	15	9	2	4
2	12	6	7	8	0	4	1
4	4	0	6	7	9	5	3
9	5	12	6	6	1	8	1
13	8	11	9	10	1	12	5

Name _____ Date _____

The Dice Game

Roll three dice. Start with the number on one of the dice. Add or subtract the numbers on each of the other dice. Can you find your answer below? Color it in. Can you get four in a row?

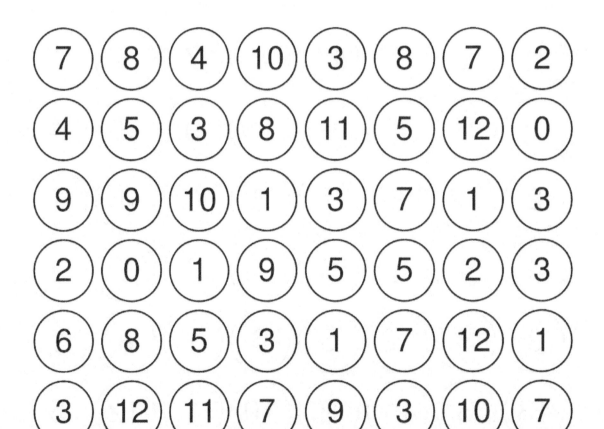

7   8   4   10   3   8   7   2

4   5   3   8   11   5   12   0

9   9   10   1   3   7   1   3

2   0   1   9   5   5   2   3

6   8   5   3   1   7   12   1

3   12   11   7   9   3   10   7

The Dice Game

Roll three dice. Start with the number on one of the dice. Add or subtract the numbers on each of the other dice. Can you find your answer below? Color it in. Can you get four in a row?

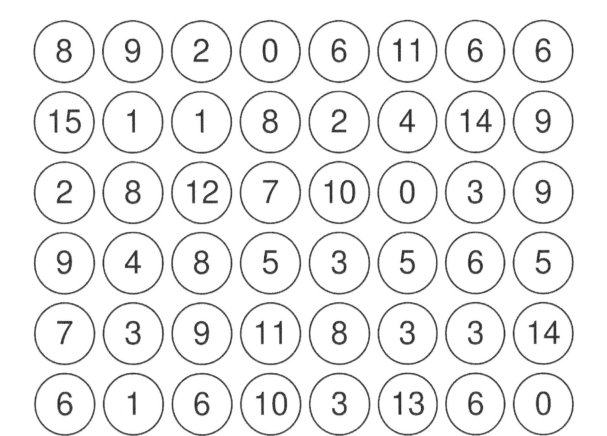

The Dice Game

Roll three dice. Start with the number on one of the dice. Add or subtract the numbers on each of the other dice. Can you find your answer below? Color it in. Can you get four in a row?

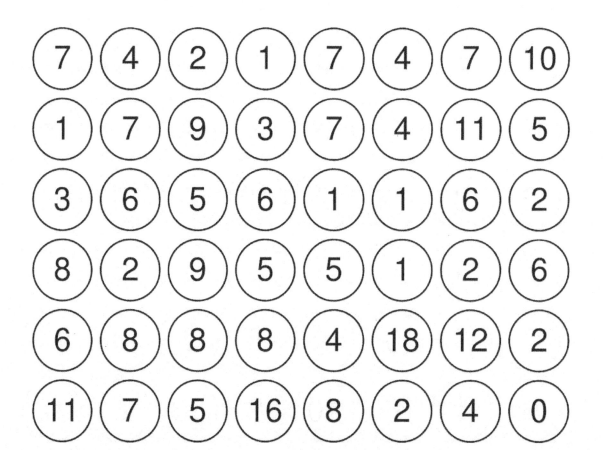

The Dice Game

Roll three dice. Start with the number on one of the dice. Add or subtract the numbers on each of the other dice. Can you find your answer below? Color it in. Can you get four in a row?

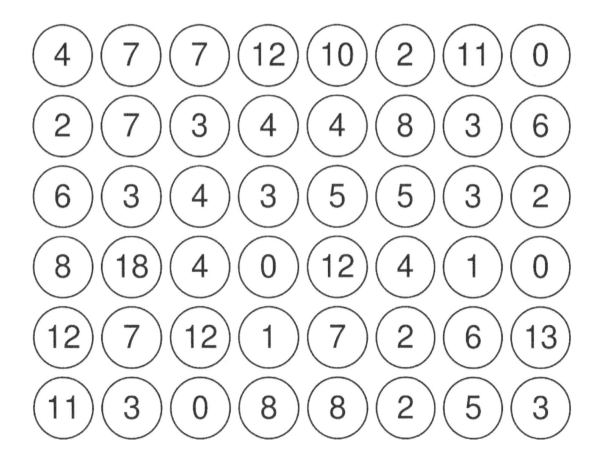

4	7	7	12	10	2	11	0
2	7	3	4	4	8	3	6
6	3	4	3	5	5	3	2
8	18	4	0	12	4	1	0
12	7	12	1	7	2	6	13
11	3	0	8	8	2	5	3

The Dice Game

Roll four dice. Start with the number on one of the dice. Add or subtract the numbers on each of the other dice. Can you find your answer below? Color it in. Can you get four in a row?

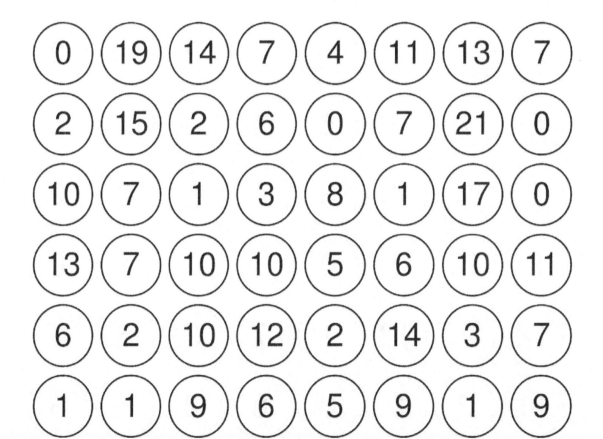

0 19 14 7 4 11 13 7

2 15 2 6 0 7 21 0

10 7 1 3 8 1 17 0

13 7 10 10 5 6 10 11

6 2 10 12 2 14 3 7

1 1 9 6 5 9 1 9

Name _____ Date _____

The Dice Game

Roll four dice. Start with the number on one of the dice. Add or subtract the numbers on each of the other dice. Can you find your answer below? Color it in. Can you get four in a row?

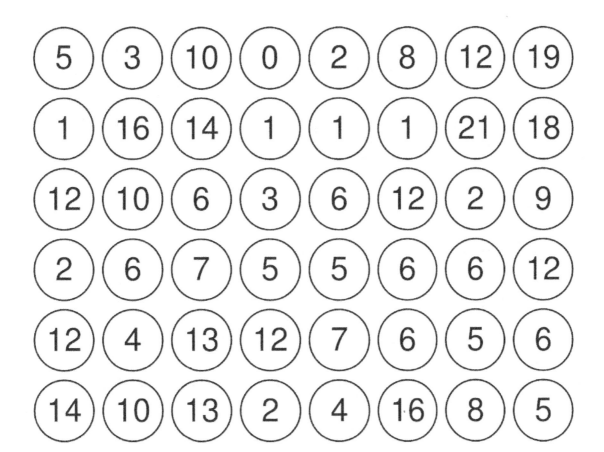

5 3 10 0 2 8 12 19

1 16 14 1 1 1 21 18

12 10 6 3 6 12 2 9

2 6 7 5 5 6 6 12

12 4 13 12 7 6 5 6

14 10 13 2 4 16 8 5

Name _____ Date _____

The Dice Game

Roll four dice. Start with the number on one of the dice. Add or subtract the numbers on each of the other dice. Can you find your answer below? Color it in. Can you get four in a row?

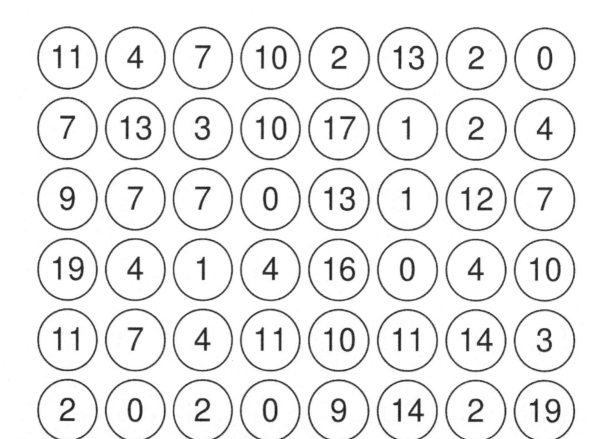

11	4	7	10	2	13	2	0
7	13	3	10	17	1	2	4
9	7	7	0	13	1	12	7
19	4	1	4	16	0	4	10
11	7	4	11	10	11	14	3
2	0	2	0	9	14	2	19

The Dice Game

Roll four dice. Start with the number on one of the dice. Add or subtract the numbers on each of the other dice. Can you find your answer below? Color it in. Can you get four in a row?

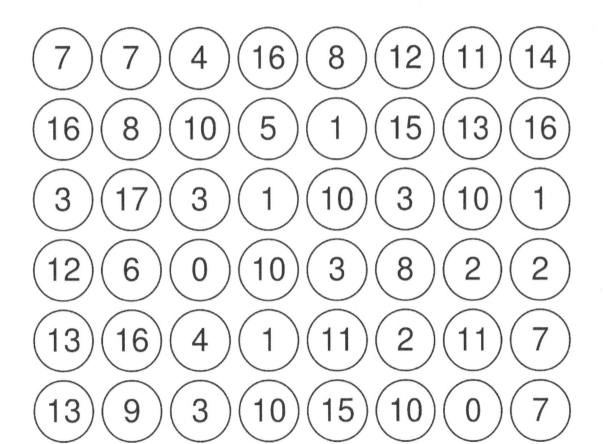

Name _____ Date _____

The Dice Game

Roll four dice. Start with the number on one of the dice. Add or subtract the numbers on each of the other dice. Can you find your answer below? Color it in. Can you get four in a row?

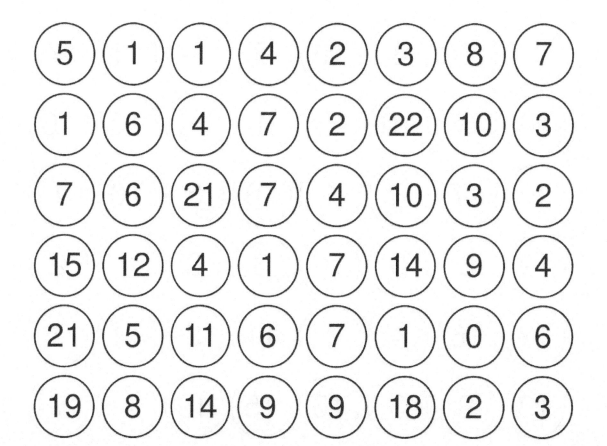

5	1	1	4	2	3	8	7
1	6	4	7	2	22	10	3
7	6	21	7	4	10	3	2
15	12	4	1	7	14	9	4
21	5	11	6	7	1	0	6
19	8	14	9	9	18	2	3

The Dice Game

Roll four dice. Start with the number on one of the dice. Add or subtract the numbers on each of the other dice. Can you find your answer below? Color it in. Can you get four in a row?

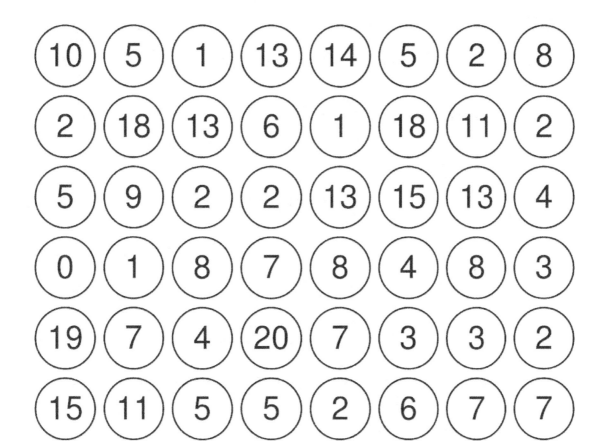

10	5	1	13	14	5	2	8
2	18	13	6	1	18	11	2
5	9	2	2	13	15	13	4
0	1	8	7	8	4	8	3
19	7	4	20	7	3	3	2
15	11	5	5	2	6	7	7

The Dice Game

Roll four dice. Start with the number on one of the dice. Add or subtract the numbers on each of the other dice. Can you find your answer below? Color it in. Can you get four in a row?

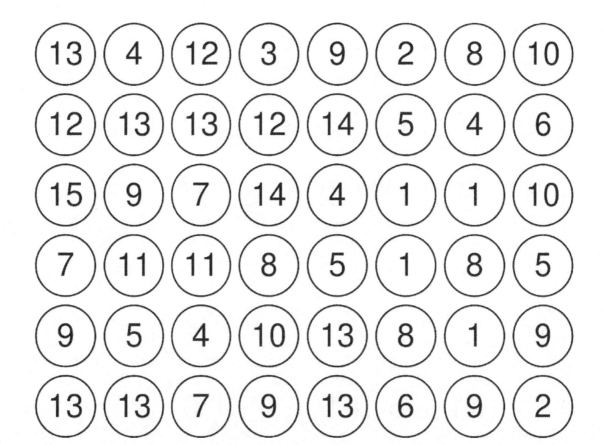

The Dice Game

Roll four dice. Start with the number on one of the dice. Add or subtract the numbers on each of the other dice. Can you find your answer below? Color it in. Can you get four in a row?

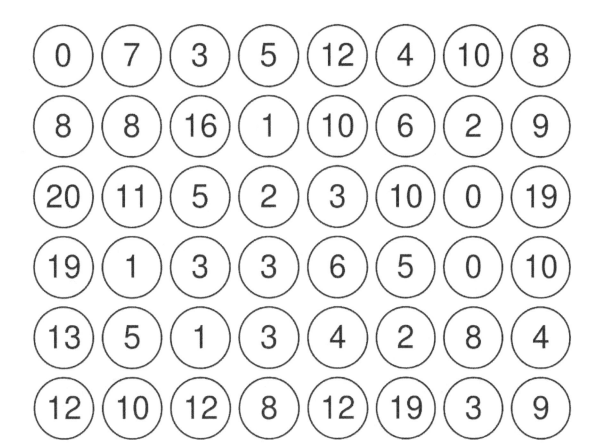

The Dice Game

Roll four dice. Start with the number on one of the dice. Add or subtract the numbers on each of the other dice. Can you find your answer below? Color it in. Can you get four in a row?

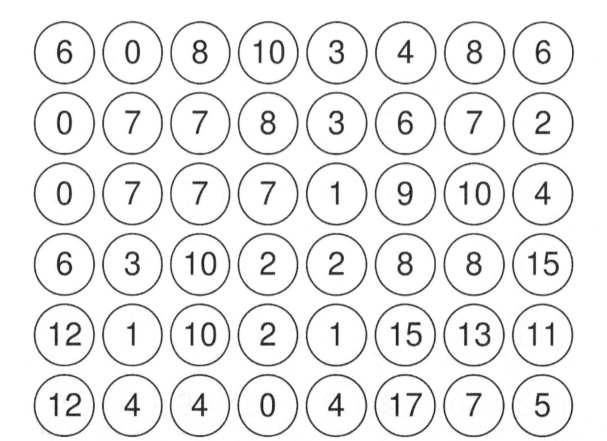

The Dice Game

Roll four dice. Start with the number on one of the dice. Add or subtract the numbers on each of the other dice. Can you find your answer below? Color it in. Can you get four in a row?

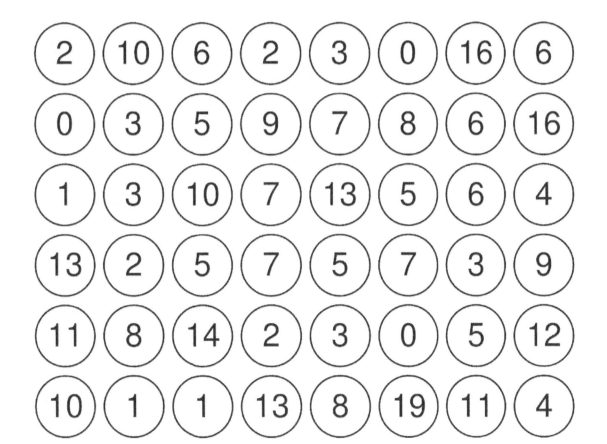

2	10	6	2	3	0	16	6
0	3	5	9	7	8	6	16
1	3	10	7	13	5	6	4
13	2	5	7	5	7	3	9
11	8	14	2	3	0	5	12
10	1	1	13	8	19	11	4

Name _____ Date _____

The Dice Game

Roll four dice. Start with the number on one of the dice. Add or subtract the numbers on each of the other dice. Can you find your answer below? Color it in. Can you get four in a row?

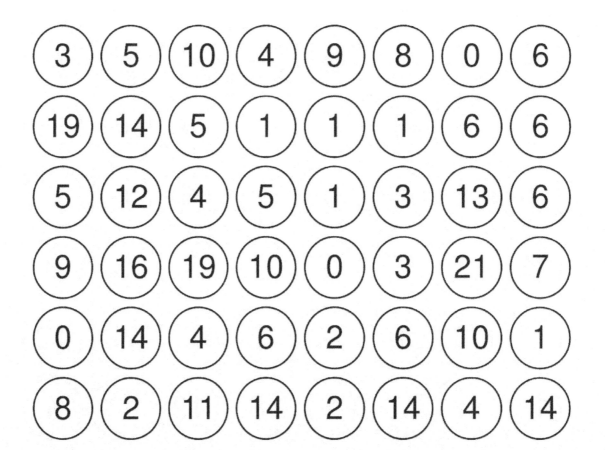

3	5	10	4	9	8	0	6
19	14	5	1	1	1	6	6
5	12	4	5	1	3	13	6
9	16	19	10	0	3	21	7
0	14	4	6	2	6	10	1
8	2	11	14	2	14	4	14

The Dice Game

Roll four dice. Start with the number on one of the dice. Add or subtract the numbers on each of the other dice. Can you find your answer below? Color it in. Can you get four in a row?

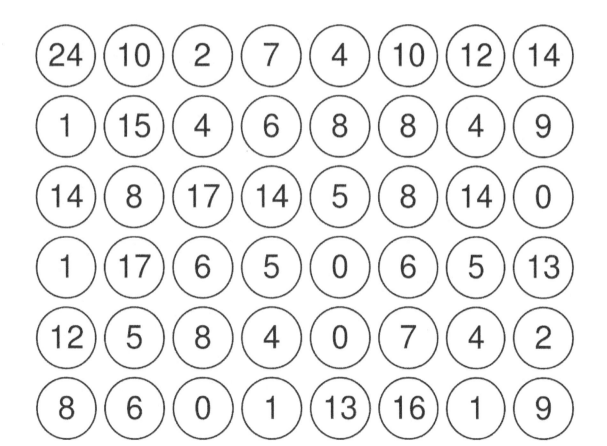

Name _____ Date _____

The Dice Game

Roll four dice. Start with the number on one of the dice. Add or subtract the numbers on each of the other dice. Can you find your answer below? Color it in. Can you get four in a row?

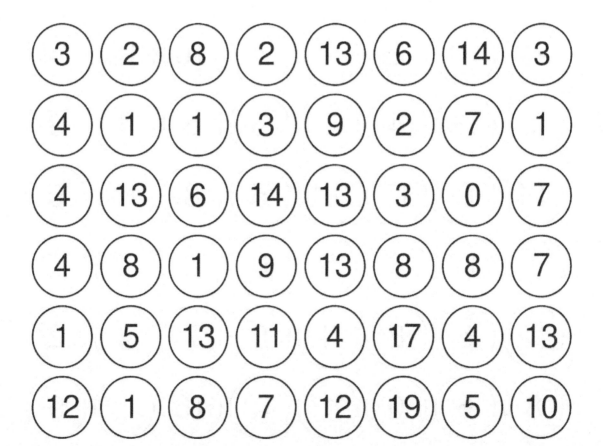

3	2	8	2	13	6	14	3
4	1	1	3	9	2	7	1
4	13	6	14	13	3	0	7
4	8	1	9	13	8	8	7
1	5	13	11	4	17	4	13
12	1	8	7	12	19	5	10

The Dice Game

Roll four dice. Start with the number on one of the dice. Add or subtract the numbers on each of the other dice. Can you find your answer below? Color it in. Can you get four in a row?

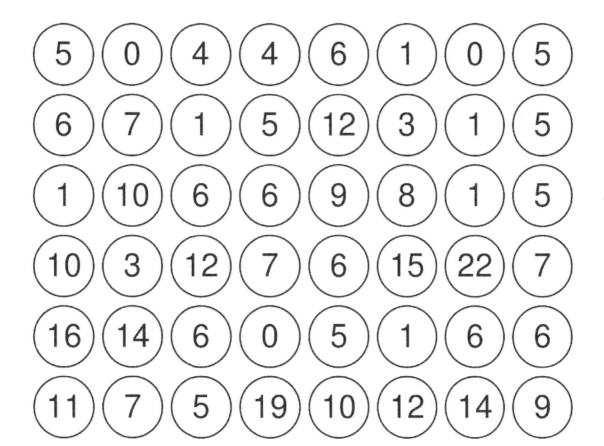

5	0	4	4	6	1	0	5
6	7	1	5	12	3	1	5
1	10	6	6	9	8	1	5
10	3	12	7	6	15	22	7
16	14	6	0	5	1	6	6
11	7	5	19	10	12	14	9

Name _____ Date _____

The Dice Game

Roll four dice. Start with the number on one of the dice. Add or subtract the numbers on each of the other dice. Can you find your answer below? Color it in. Can you get four in a row?

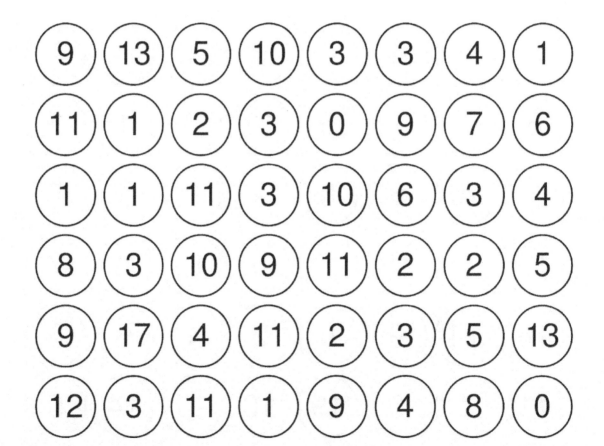

9 13 5 10 3 3 4 1

11 1 2 3 0 9 7 6

1 1 11 3 10 6 3 4

8 3 10 9 11 2 2 5

9 17 4 11 2 3 5 13

12 3 11 1 9 4 8 0

The Dice Game

Roll four dice. Start with the number on one of the dice. Add or subtract the numbers on each of the other dice. Can you find your answer below? Color it in. Can you get four in a row?

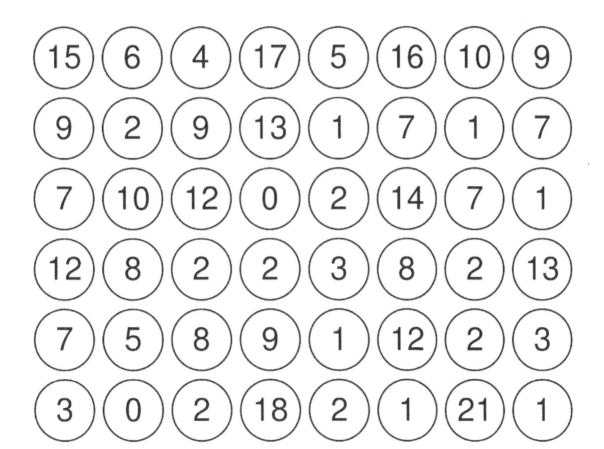

15	6	4	17	5	16	10	9
9	2	9	13	1	7	1	7
7	10	12	0	2	14	7	1
12	8	2	2	3	8	2	13
7	5	8	9	1	12	2	3
3	0	2	18	2	1	21	1

Name _____ Date _____

The Dice Game

Roll four dice. Start with the number on one of the dice. Add or subtract the numbers on each of the other dice. Can you find your answer below? Color it in. Can you get four in a row?

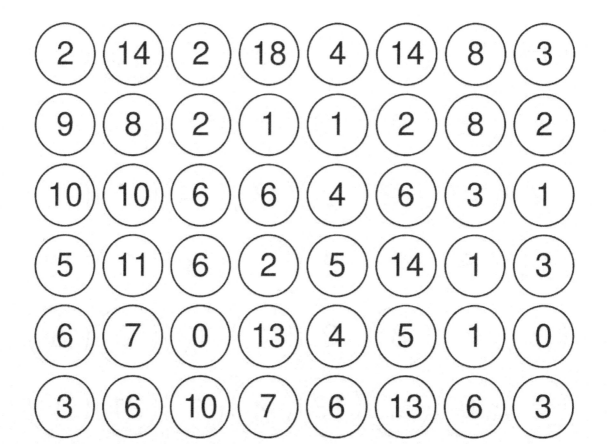

2 14 2 18 4 14 8 3

9 8 2 1 1 2 8 2

10 10 6 6 4 6 3 1

5 11 6 2 5 14 1 3

6 7 0 13 4 5 1 0

3 6 10 7 6 13 6 3

The Dice Game

Roll four dice. Start with the number on one of the dice. Add or subtract the numbers on each of the other dice. Can you find your answer below? Color it in. Can you get four in a row?

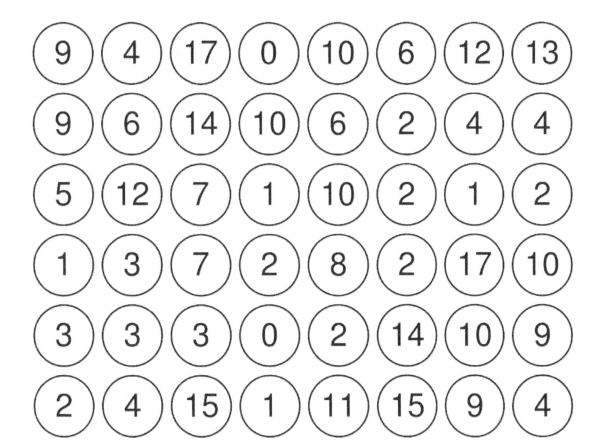

9	4	17	0	10	6	12	13
9	6	14	10	6	2	4	4
5	12	7	1	10	2	1	2
1	3	7	2	8	2	17	10
3	3	3	0	2	14	10	9
2	4	15	1	11	15	9	4

Name _____ Date _____

The Dice Game

Roll four dice. Start with the number on one of the dice. Add or subtract the numbers on each of the other dice. Can you find your answer below? Color it in. Can you get four in a row?

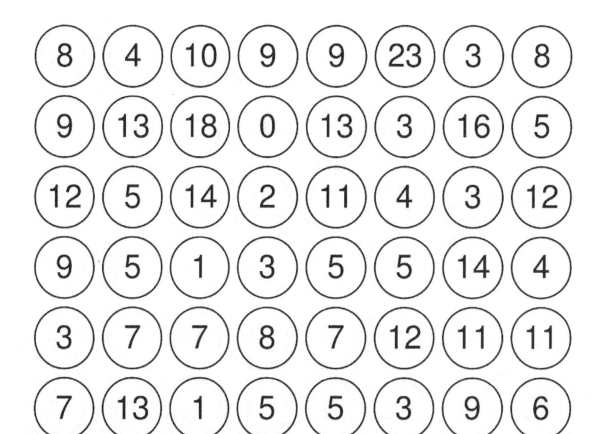

The Dice Game

Roll four dice. Start with the number on one of the dice. Add or subtract the numbers on each of the other dice. Can you find your answer below? Color it in. Can you get four in a row?

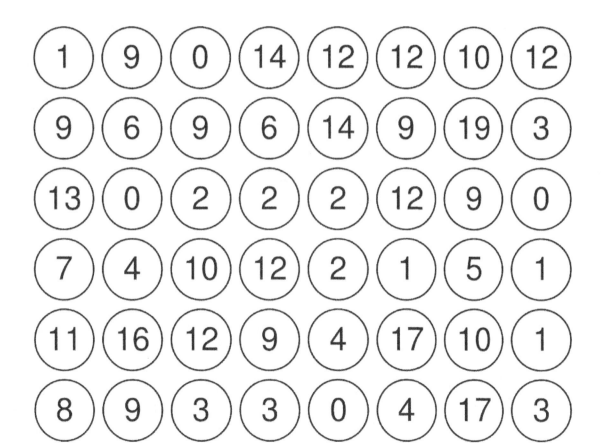

Name _____ Date _____

The Dice Game

Roll four dice. Start with the number on one of the dice. Add or subtract the numbers on each of the other dice. Can you find your answer below? Color it in. Can you get four in a row?

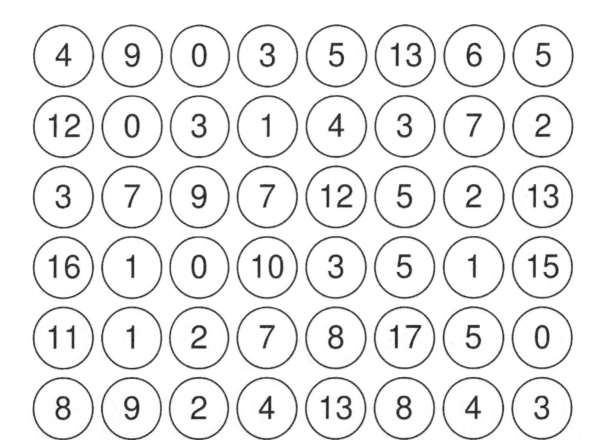

4　9　0　3　5　13　6　5

12　0　3　1　4　3　7　2

3　7　9　7　12　5　2　13

16　1　0　10　3　5　1　15

11　1　2　7　8　17　5　0

8　9　2　4　13　8　4　3

Name _____ Date _____

The Dice Game

Roll four dice. Start with the number on one of the dice. Add or subtract the numbers on each of the other dice. Can you find your answer below? Color it in. Can you get four in a row?

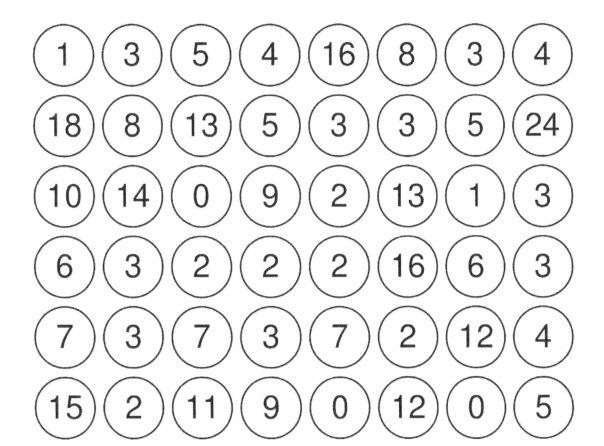

1	3	5	4	16	8	3	4
18	8	13	5	3	3	5	24
10	14	0	9	2	13	1	3
6	3	2	2	2	16	6	3
7	3	7	3	7	2	12	4
15	2	11	9	0	12	0	5

The Dice Game

Roll four dice. Start with the number on one of the dice. Add or subtract the numbers on each of the other dice. Can you find your answer below? Color it in. Can you get four in a row?

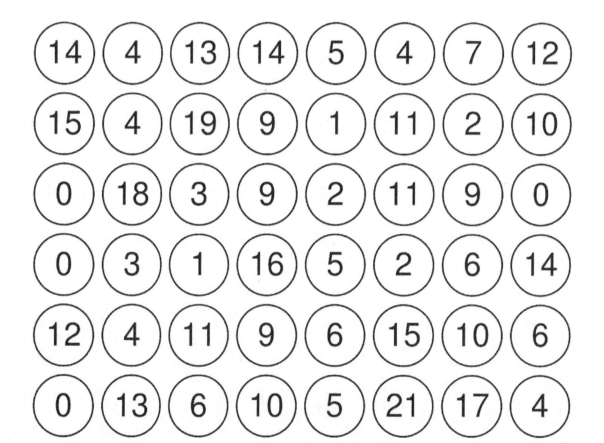

The Dice Game

Roll four dice. Start with the number on one of the dice. Add or subtract the numbers on each of the other dice. Can you find your answer below? Color it in. Can you get four in a row?

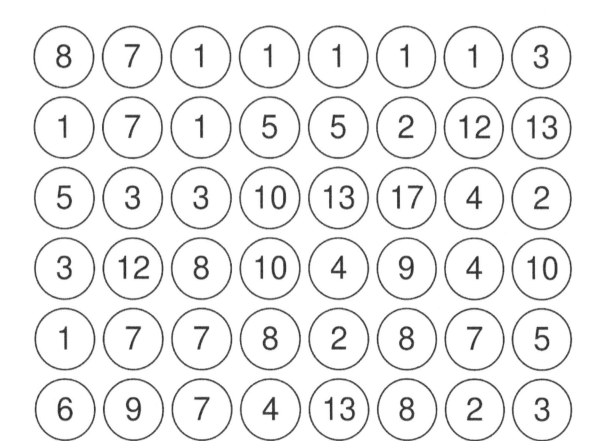

The Dice Game

Roll four dice. Start with the number on one of the dice. Add or subtract the numbers on each of the other dice. Can you find your answer below? Color it in. Can you get four in a row?

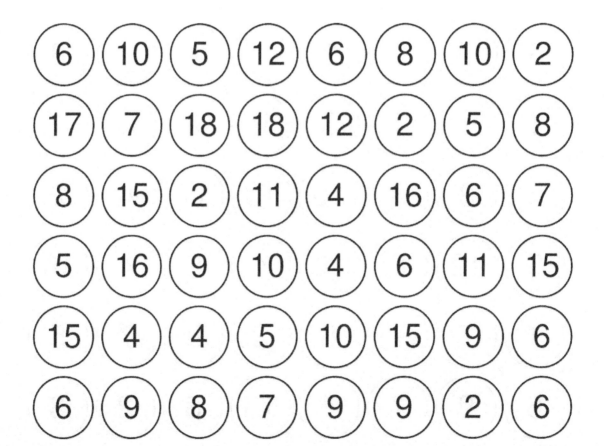

6 10 5 12 6 8 10 2

17 7 18 18 12 2 5 8

8 15 2 11 4 16 6 7

5 16 9 10 4 6 11 15

15 4 4 5 10 15 9 6

6 9 8 7 9 9 2 6

The Dice Game

Roll four dice. Start with the number on one of the dice. Add or subtract the numbers on each of the other dice. Can you find your answer below? Color it in. Can you get four in a row?

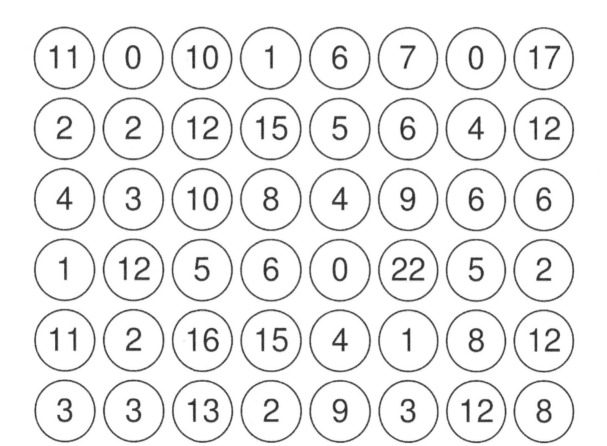

11	0	10	1	6	7	0	17
2	2	12	15	5	6	4	12
4	3	10	8	4	9	6	6
1	12	5	6	0	22	5	2
11	2	16	15	4	1	8	12
3	3	13	2	9	3	12	8

The Dice Game

Roll four dice. Start with the number on one of the dice. Add or subtract the numbers on each of the other dice. Can you find your answer below? Color it in. Can you get four in a row?

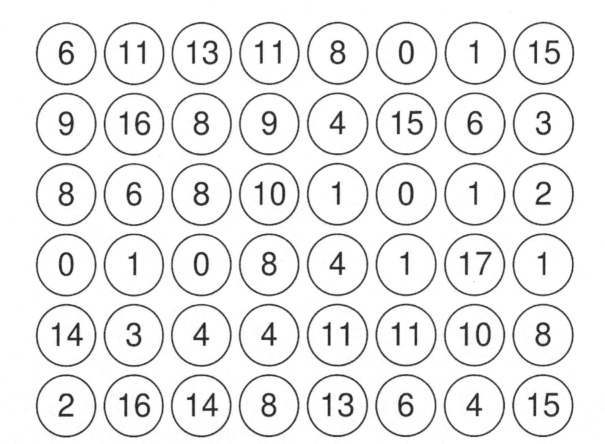

The Dice Game

Roll four dice. Start with the number on one of the dice. Add or subtract the numbers on each of the other dice. Can you find your answer below? Color it in. Can you get four in a row?

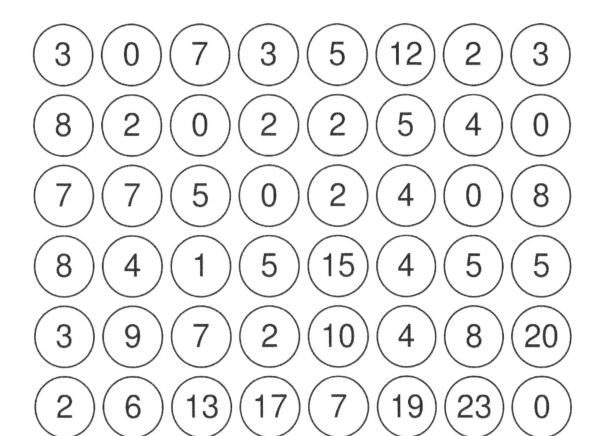

The Dice Game

Roll four dice. Start with the
number on one of the dice.
Add or subtract the
numbers on each of the
other dice. Can you find
your answer below? Color it
in. Can you get four in a
row?

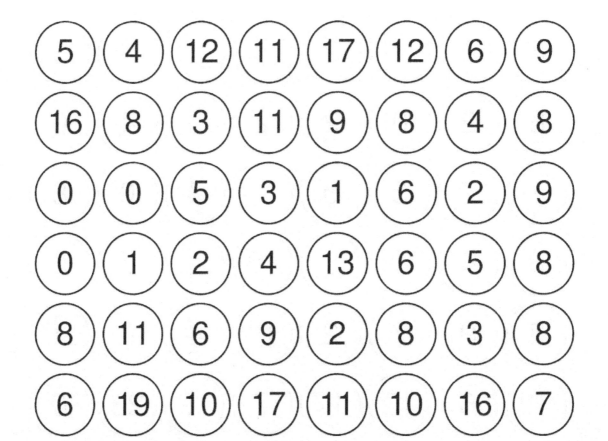

5	4	12	11	17	12	6	9
16	8	3	11	9	8	4	8
0	0	5	3	1	6	2	9
0	1	2	4	13	6	5	8
8	11	6	9	2	8	3	8
6	19	10	17	11	10	16	7

The Dice Game

Roll four dice. Start with the number on one of the dice. Add or subtract the numbers on each of the other dice. Can you find your answer below? Color it in. Can you get four in a row?

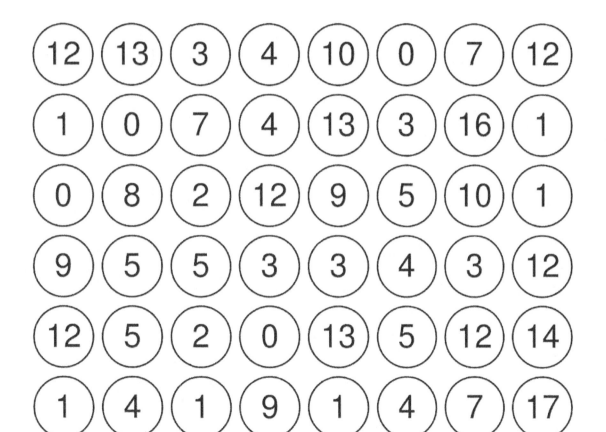

12 13 3 4 10 0 7 12

1 0 7 4 13 3 16 1

0 8 2 12 9 5 10 1

9 5 5 3 3 4 3 12

12 5 2 0 13 5 12 14

1 4 1 9 1 4 7 17

The Dice Game

Roll four dice. Start with the number on one of the dice. Add or subtract the numbers on each of the other dice. Can you find your answer below? Color it in. Can you get four in a row?

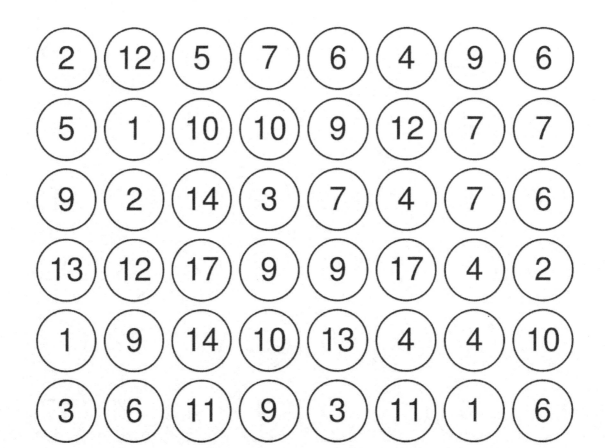

The Dice Game

Roll four dice. Start with the number on one of the dice. Add or subtract the numbers on each of the other dice. Can you find your answer below? Color it in. Can you get four in a row?

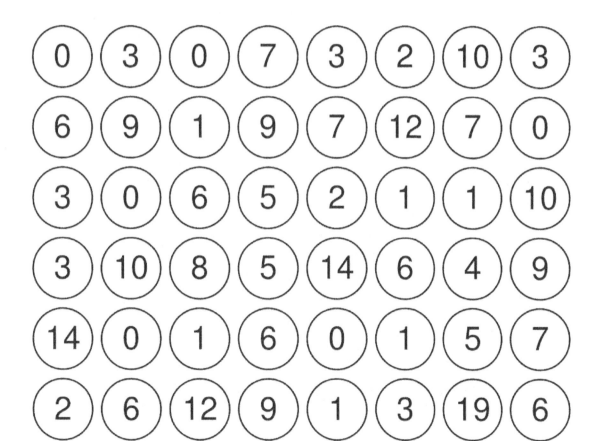

Name _____ Date _____

The Dice Game

Roll four dice. Start with the number on one of the dice. Add or subtract the numbers on each of the other dice. Can you find your answer below? Color it in. Can you get four in a row?

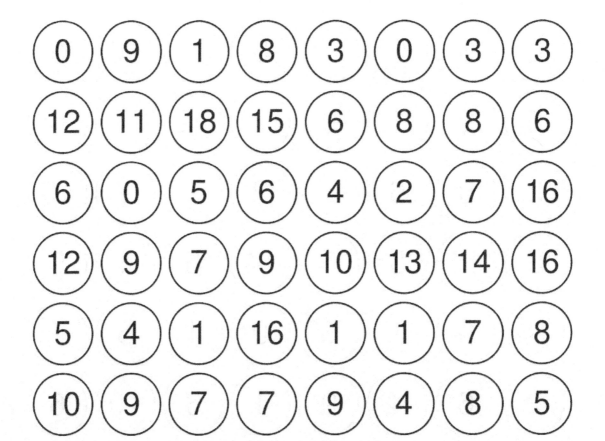

0	9	1	8	3	0	3	3
12	11	18	15	6	8	8	6
6	0	5	6	4	2	7	16
12	9	7	9	10	13	14	16
5	4	1	16	1	1	7	8
10	9	7	7	9	4	8	5

The Dice Game

Roll four dice. Start with the number on one of the dice. Add or subtract the numbers on each of the other dice. Can you find your answer below? Color it in. Can you get four in a row?

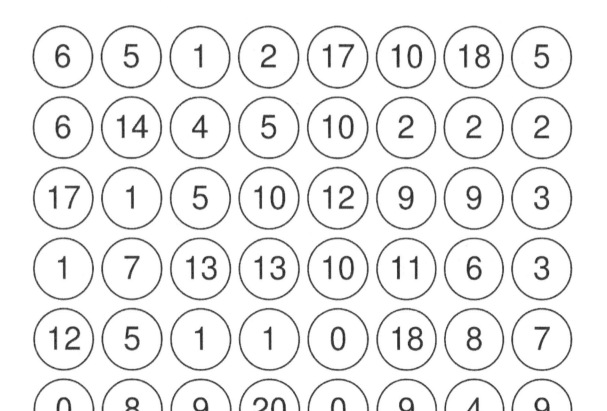

The Dice Game

Roll four dice. Start with the number on one of the dice. Add or subtract the numbers on each of the other dice. Can you find your answer below? Color it in. Can you get four in a row?

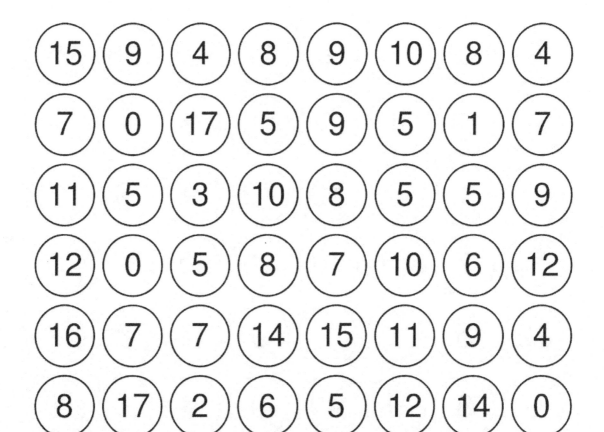

The Dice Game

Roll four dice. Start with the number on one of the dice. Add or subtract the numbers on each of the other dice. Can you find your answer below? Color it in. Can you get four in a row?

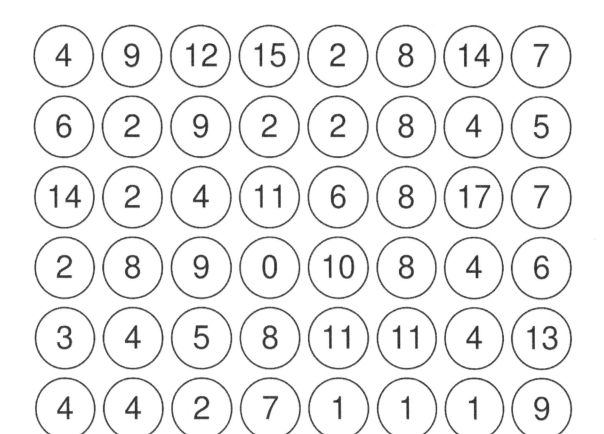

The Dice Game

Roll four dice. Start with the number on one of the dice. Add or subtract the numbers on each of the other dice. Can you find your answer below? Color it in. Can you get four in a row?

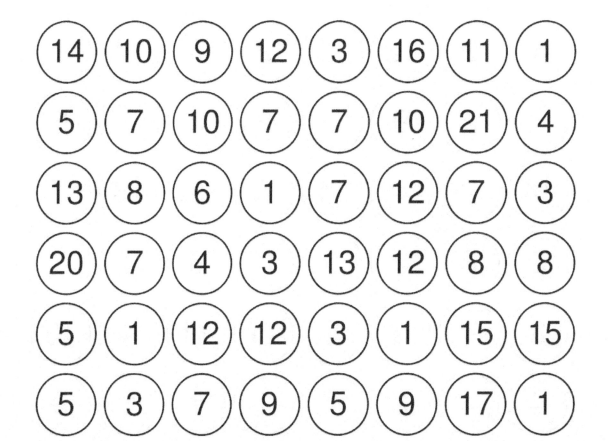

Name _____ Date _____

The Dice Game

Roll four dice. Start with the number on one of the dice. Add or subtract the numbers on each of the other dice. Can you find your answer below? Color it in. Can you get four in a row?

16	2	13	23	2	5	4	4
2	1	15	4	5	4	5	10
0	3	7	3	9	1	16	1
4	0	11	5	13	7	2	4
13	1	4	16	6	1	4	11
8	12	3	14	15	7	0	10

The Dice Game

Roll four dice. Start with the number on one of the dice. Add or subtract the numbers on each of the other dice. Can you find your answer below? Color it in. Can you get four in a row?

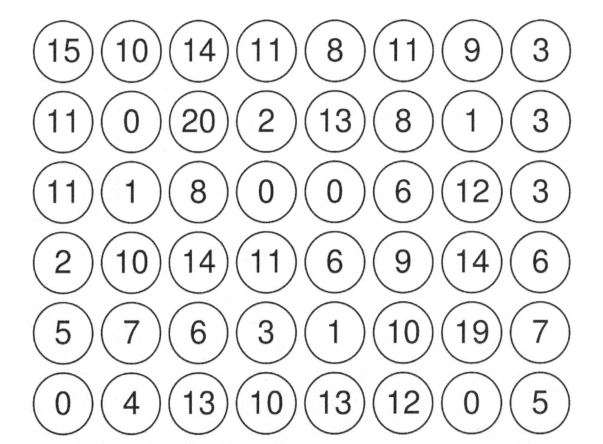

The Dice Game

Roll four dice. Start with the number on one of the dice. Add or subtract the numbers on each of the other dice. Can you find your answer below? Color it in. Can you get four in a row?

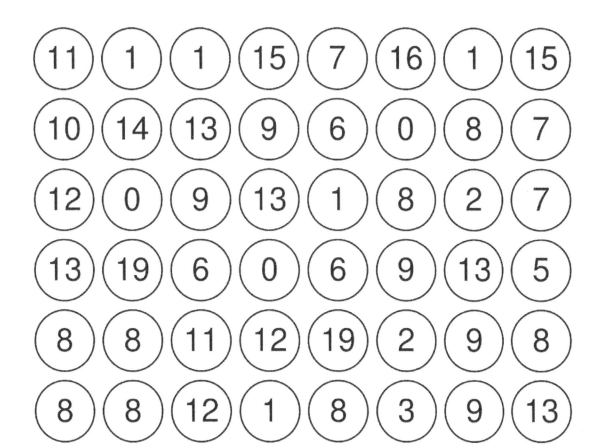

11 1 1 15 7 16 1 15

10 14 13 9 6 0 8 7

12 0 9 13 1 8 2 7

13 19 6 0 6 9 13 5

8 8 11 12 19 2 9 8

8 8 12 1 8 3 9 13

The Dice Game

Roll four dice. Start with the number on one of the dice. Add or subtract the numbers on each of the other dice. Can you find your answer below? Color it in. Can you get four in a row?

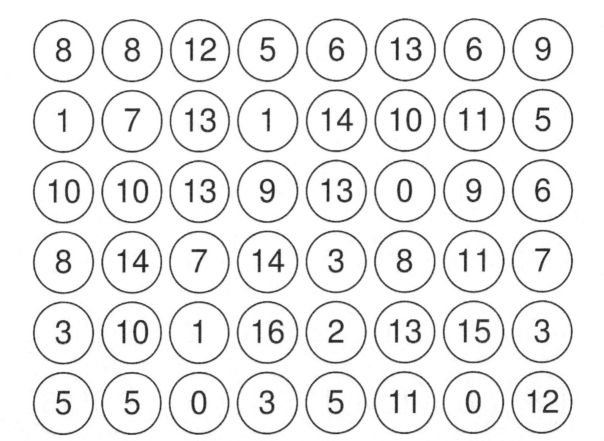

The numbers in the circles are:

8 8 12 5 6 13 6 9

1 7 13 1 14 10 11 5

10 10 13 9 13 0 9 6

8 14 7 14 3 8 11 7

3 10 1 16 2 13 15 3

5 5 0 3 5 11 0 12

The Dice Game

Roll four dice. Start with the number on one of the dice. Add or subtract the numbers on each of the other dice. Can you find your answer below? Color it in. Can you get four in a row?

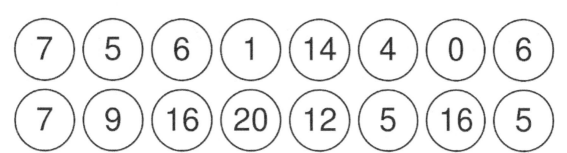

7	5	6	1	14	4	0	6
7	9	16	20	12	5	16	5
4	14	4	14	9	3	13	7
0	4	5	13	14	4	7	0
12	1	7	8	14	8	6	13
5	9	2	12	3	10	9	16

The Dice Game

Roll four dice. Start with the number on one of the dice. Add or subtract the numbers on each of the other dice. Can you find your answer below? Color it in. Can you get four in a row?

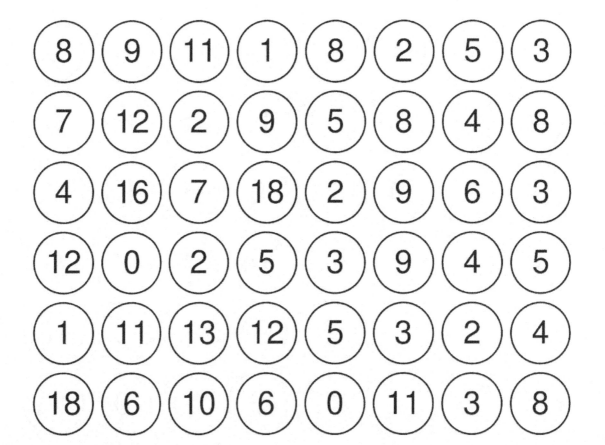

8	9	11	1	8	2	5	3
7	12	2	9	5	8	4	8
4	16	7	18	2	9	6	3
12	0	2	5	3	9	4	5
1	11	13	12	5	3	2	4
18	6	10	6	0	11	3	8

The Dice Game

Roll four dice. Start with the number on one of the dice. Add or subtract the numbers on each of the other dice. Can you find your answer below? Color it in. Can you get four in a row?

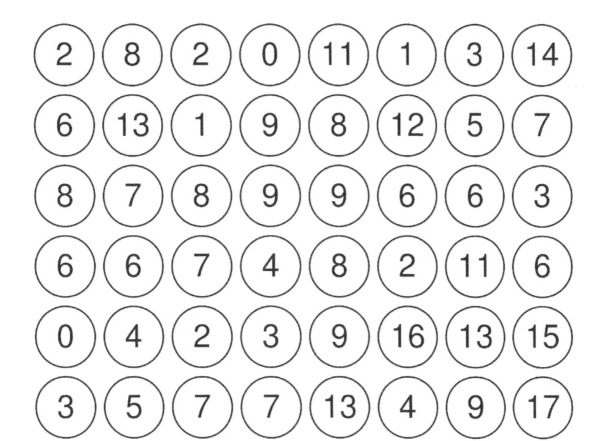

2	8	2	0	11	1	3	14
6	13	1	9	8	12	5	7
8	7	8	9	9	6	6	3
6	6	7	4	8	2	11	6
0	4	2	3	9	16	13	15
3	5	7	7	13	4	9	17

The Dice Game

Roll four dice. Start with the number on one of the dice. Add or subtract the numbers on each of the other dice. Can you find your answer below? Color it in. Can you get four in a row?

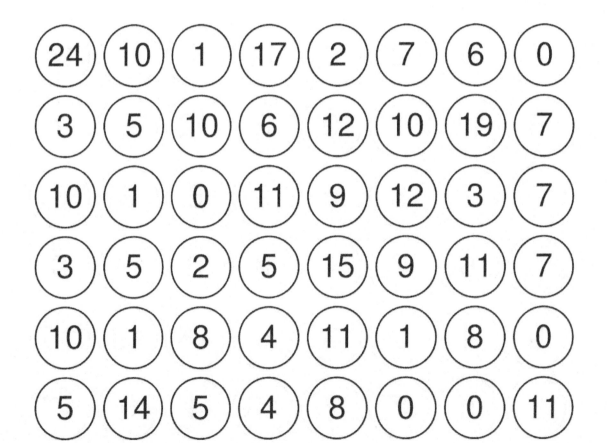

24	10	1	17	2	7	6	0
3	5	10	6	12	10	19	7
10	1	0	11	9	12	3	7
3	5	2	5	15	9	11	7
10	1	8	4	11	1	8	0
5	14	5	4	8	0	0	11

The Dice Game

Roll four dice. Start with the number on one of the dice. Add or subtract the numbers on each of the other dice. Can you find your answer below? Color it in. Can you get four in a row?

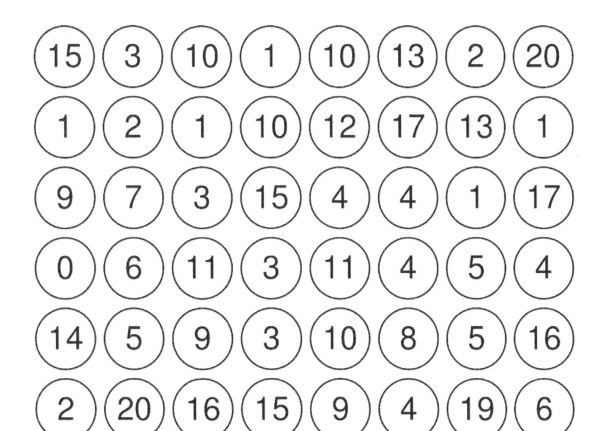

The Dice Game

Roll four dice. Start with the number on one of the dice. Add or subtract the numbers on each of the other dice. Can you find your answer below? Color it in. Can you get four in a row?

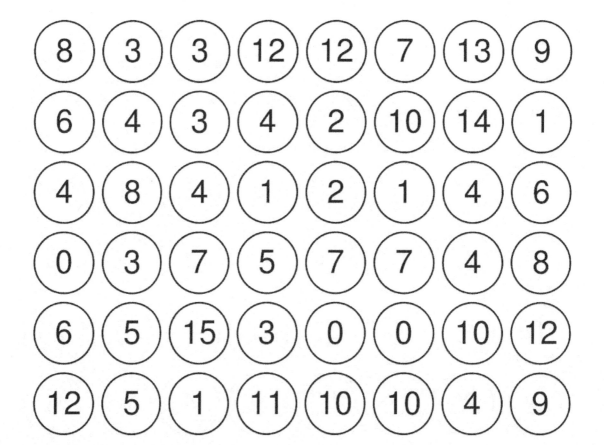

The Dice Game

Roll four dice. Start with the number on one of the dice. Add or subtract the numbers on each of the other dice. Can you find your answer below? Color it in. Can you get four in a row?

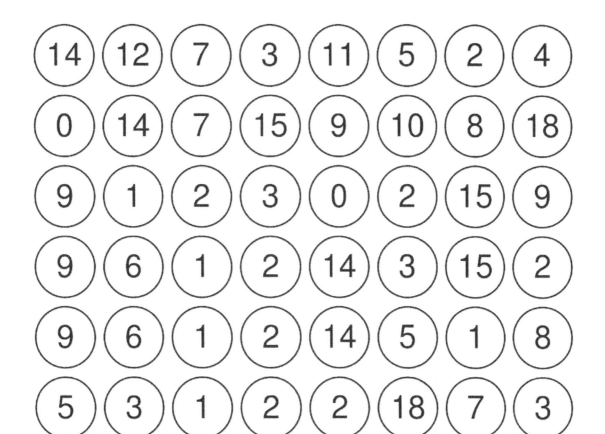

The Dice Game

Roll four dice. Start with the number on one of the dice. Add or subtract the numbers on each of the other dice. Can you find your answer below? Color it in. Can you get four in a row?

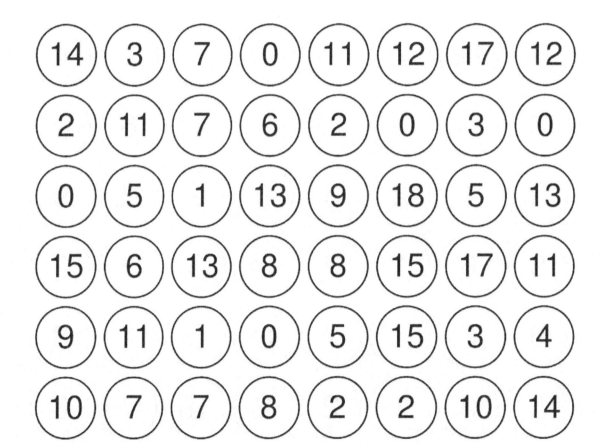

14	3	7	0	11	12	17	12
2	11	7	6	2	0	3	0
0	5	1	13	9	18	5	13
15	6	13	8	8	15	17	11
9	11	1	0	5	15	3	4
10	7	7	8	2	2	10	14

The Dice Game

Roll four dice. Start with the number on one of the dice. Add or subtract the numbers on each of the other dice. Can you find your answer below? Color it in. Can you get four in a row?

4	12	16	23	2	14	7	9
1	2	8	6	16	8	3	7
9	9	8	14	4	14	0	12
9	11	9	1	11	3	0	13
13	20	2	8	9	13	2	11
4	13	4	16	12	3	8	6

Made in the USA
Monee, IL
23 August 2022